THE TIME SELLER

JOSSEY-BASS

The Time Seller

A BUSINESS SATIRE

Fernando Trías de Bes

BICENTENNIAL
1807
WILEY
2007
BICENTENNIAL

John Wiley & Sons, Inc.

Published by Jossey-Bass
A Wiley Imprint
989 Market Street, San Francisco, CA 94103-1741   www.josseybass.com

Library of Congress Cataloging-in-Publication Data

Trías de Bes, Fernando.
   The time seller : a business satire / by Fernando Trías de Bes.
      p. cm.
   ISBN-13: 978-0-7879-8838-8
   ISBN-10: 0-7879-8838-3
   1. Business—Fiction. 2. Time—Fiction. 3. Satire. I. Title.
   PS3620.R53T46 2007
   813'.6—dc22

                                        2006029701

Printed in the United States of America
FIRST EDITION
HB Printing   10 9 8 7 6 5 4 3 2 1

CONTENTS

To my son Alejo,
with all my love,
in case I am unable to communicate to him
that his time is his alone.

Prologue

People have little time to read. So, dear reader, imagine how little remains for one to write. These are reasons of sufficient weight to sway me in favor of writing this story in its abbreviated version; it's more practical for all.

To that end, I looked up the word *abbreviate* in the dictionary, and the definition appears as follows:

Abbreviate: v. tr. To shorten (a word, phrase, or text).

In other words, an abbreviated novel should shorten the story it tells in time and space. The written text occupies less paper, and it takes the reader less time to read.

Therefore, hereafter I shall use the letter "T" to refer to the word *time.* For money, I shall employ the character $. That simplifies things. There's an old Spanish saying that goes: "Time is gold." In English, "Time is money." So, in this new format that I have just invented, the adage is written thus:

"T is $."

But, in an abbreviating mood, let us begin by ending this Prologue here and moving on to Chapter One, which we shall abbreviate as C1. No doubt you haven't much time—sorry, T—either.

Alll events recounted here happened to an average Guy who lived in a place called the Unnamed Settled Area. We shall use his initials—AG—but not those of his native land, for our setting would no longer be unnamed.

From a very early age AG took a keen interest in the reproductive system of the red-headed termite (that is, Rd-Hded Trmte). Back in grade school, AG's natural sciences teacher had been explaining how mammals reproduced the day before the elevator in his apartment building fell from the fifth floor, with him in it. Miraculously, the teacher wasn't hurt, but the shock gave him jaundice, in addition to an incurable stutter, which slowed progress on the curriculum considerably for AG and his classmates. What they had been covering in a week now took four and, obviously, there was no T to finish the entire program or even get to the chapter on the reproductive system of the Rd-Hded Trmte, which was what interested AG most. And since doubt stirs curiosity, he then acquired such a longing to know about the Trmtes that he never managed to get them out of his head.

AG finished his years of compulsory education with his sights set on pursuing a career as an entomologist, thus

to devote himself heart and soul to his insects. He applied
to university as a biology major but didn't have the grades.

AG was demoralized and disappointed. The blow
struck with the force of a wrecking ball. No matter how
hard he tried, he never understood why his grades in
Latin, Greek, calculus, and art history should deny him the
chance to study insects. But that's the way things worked
in the Unnamed Settled Area.

With Trmtes out, there was nothing to do but what
his father told him to do: accounting. AG got his accounting degree at the early age of twenty-two. Upon seeing the
diploma, his father hugged him as he addressed his wife.

"Our son counts now, dear," he said snidely.

His father's remark irked AG for two reasons. First
because his mother had been deeply moved by the
diploma and then because, actually, he planned to forget
about accounting and specialize in terrarium construction.
Building and stocking Trmte terraria was a challenging
discipline and there were but a handful of specialists in the
country, which heralded a brilliant future and the chance
to return to the professional path he'd always wanted to
follow. However, once again something got between him
and the Rd-Hded Trmte: matrimony.

There's no need to spend T or space on giving details
about AG's wife. There's no T for that. So, as I did with AG,
I shall skip her description. Let the reader decide her age,

her job, if she is to be fair or dark, if her character is sweet or rebellious. I couldn't care less. We'll call her AG's wife. To abbreviate, hereafter, she'll be AGW.

Now, by not telling of AGW's childhood and how she met and fell in love with AG we have succeeded in saving about six pages and your interest in this story has not diminished one bit, not yet.

AG and AGW got married in a simple, intimate ceremony. Among the guests were his grade school teacher, who failed to finish his toast, for his stutter had only worsened since his fall in the elevator. After a brief honeymoon, AG and his new wife focused their efforts on the search for a place to live. They looked first at large, centrally located apartments—"How much did you say for this place?"—then midsized and on the edge of town—"Sorry, what was that price again?"—then much smaller digs, quite a ways out of town—"Are you sure you have the price right?" They finally bought a miserable little apartment of six hundred and fifty square feet (a thousand to friends).

They added a parking space in the garage to their purchase, and thus could not afford a storage space. Then their first child was born, whom we shall call AG-1. Five years later the second, AG-2, came along, and after another four years a miserable AGW complained to her husband:

"If we had a storage space, we could have a third child, but with so few closets, we don't have room for clothes for five. Now, all the storage spaces in the building are taken. What will become of us?"

She wept bitterly. AG would never have imagined that for the want of a few square feet, years later, an entire life would be shipwrecked, for they decided to have no more children. But that's how things worked in the Unnamed Settled Area.

To pay the bills for their sixteen-point-two-five by forty feet of living space, AG joined International Business Nonsense, hereafter IBN, a decentralized, globalized multi-national, where he was dispatched to the Accounting Department.

His job was to make all bills-to-pay vanish into the company's drawers and cabinets, so that IBN's suppliers would have to send them again, thereby postponing the due date.

AG worked long and hard. He arrived at the office early; he arrived home late. On days he decided not to take the car, he spent hours on the train, and he spent hours in his car when he didn't take the train.

And why did he work such long days at such an absurd task? And why such commitment and unshakeable dedication? The primary reason for AG's dependence on IBN was the rather hefty mortgage he had to pay each month, which the bank had "generously" given him ten years earlier, and the principal of which he had paid off all of 1 percent. That was a good deal more than nothing, as the branch director always noted, each time he phoned AG to tell him that he was overdrawn again.

AG had his mortgage with the Bank of . . . But what's the difference? All banks are the same. Let's call AG's bank Bk and we'll save ourselves another paragraph.

As it was, a friend of his father-in-law's worked at this Bk, and he assured them that they were getting the mortgage of their lives, the conditions of which they would have to keep secret, so incredibly advantageous they were. Actually, they were not so advantageous as at other financial institutions, but, as AG discovered, his father-in-law took a commission from the Bk. That, however, didn't bother AG; he got his own back when AGW's father gave him the $ that he was supposed to bet for him every week on the horses. AG never laid a single wager. That way the family stayed together and the accounts balanced.

Now we can repeat it all in summary form: AG, at the age of forty, found himself married to AGW, the father of AG-1 and AG-2, with neither storage space nor AG-3, fed up at IBN and with no T for the Rd-Hded Trmtes, which were what he had come into this world for.

But let us resume our story. The whole thing began the day that AG was listening to the radio, and a doctor, a specialist in the terminally ill, said that "in the waning measures of existence, upon the precipice of death, everyone draws up the balance sheet of their life."

AG was surprised at such a claim, for he was an accountant and he knew that *balance sheets* were not done only when a company is facing liquidation. Balance sheets were done on a yearly basis, often several times in the same business year. Why should life be any different? Why should one wait till one's deathbed to do the balance sheet of one's life?

Just in case the reader is unfamiliar with the concept of a balance sheet, it consists of two columns: "Assets," which not just I but the experts abbreviate as "A," and the opposite, "Liabilities," or "L," as the same experts would have it.

A's encompass everything the company has, holds, or expects to collect. L's encompass everything it owes, its debts, and the capital that its stockholders hold in the company. In sum, A is what the company has and L is what it owes. The general idea is that A should equal L. In other words, they always come out the same, because what one has is what one owes. Which means that one cannot have anything that one doesn't owe to someone, which is an abomination. But that's how it is.

Anyway, when AG did the A & L of his life, one sleepless night, his heart palpitating, feeling like crying and throwing in the towel, he realized just how screwed up his life had turned out: stuck up that dead-end street like all of us AGs of this world, or, to be more exact, snared in the big trap that humankind has laid for itself.

He sat restless at the dining room table. First, AG listed his A, what he had: a one-thousand-, no, sorry, six-hundred-and-fifty-square-foot apartment; his parking space; a car used by himself and before that by another; his furniture; $3,100 in the Bk, and $450 under the mattress on which AGW was sleeping placidly, unaware of the somewhat unorthodox accounting exercise her husband was performing in the next room at three in the morning.

"Look how much I have! How can it be on what I make at IBN?" he asked himself.

"Ah, of course, I haven't done the L!" he answered himself.

He started his list of debts with what he owed his brother-in-law: $1,500. His brother-in-law was like all brothers-in-law, except for one notable difference: he was *AG's* brother-in-law. And everyone knows that all brothers-in-law are extremely odd beings whom no one is quite able to understand.

He'd married AG's sister four years before, and they were rather better off. With his brother-in-law, everything was bigger: his car, his home, his TV, his bank account, and his ego. He'd lent them the $1,500 when the incident with the lace curtains happened. AG insisted on hanging them himself, ignorant of the fact that they already came with the holes. He hung them upside down, and perforated the intended lower edge with a screwdriver and pruning shears in order to fit the rings through which to pass the rods. AGW watched him incredulously, unable to dissuade him from his mission. So the curtains ended up with holes through the tops and the bottoms, and had to be thrown out. AGW turned red with anger; that evening AG's boss (and his wife) were coming for dinner and AGW was horrified at the thought that they might think she and AG couldn't afford lace curtains. But they didn't have the $ to buy a second set. AGW called his brother-in-law, who in less than an hour showed up with a curtain-hanger who solved the problem for $1,500, which AG promised to pay back. He'd never had the $ to pay off the debt, something which his SOB of a brother-in-law, with viperish irony, reminded him of every time he came to visit.

"Nice curtains," he'd quip.

But that wasn't AG's only L. On top of the $1,500 for the curtains, AG owed the Bk $355,000, which was what remained to be paid on the mortgage that he'd had to take out for the purchase of his six-hundred-and-fifty-square-foot patch of planet. Therefore, his total L amounted to $356,500.

AG regarded his L and fell into thought. Was that really his debt? No. Something told him he'd better take a deeper look at the balance sheet of his life.

If he added up his and his wife's incomes and sub-
tracted their expenses for schools, gasoline, trains, food,
clothing, unsure insurance, electricity, gas, water, phone,
the Saturday movies, the Saturday movies popcorn and the
Saturday movies soft drinks (essential for quenching the
burning thirst caused by eating the popcorn), only about
$1,400 remained, exactly $1,366.22 of which disappeared
directly into the vaults of the Bk at the end of each month.
AG knew the figure by heart: month after month for one
hundred and twenty months he'd been watching how that
very same amount was removed from his account. One
thousand three hundred and sixty-six $ and twenty-two
cents. In other words, his savings capacity was zero.

AG checked his figures that same night. He would
need thirty-five years to pay off what he owed the Bk. . . .
Therefore, his debt was not a debt in $. His debt was in
time! Sorry, in T. And that, like it or not, was the way it was.

Putting it all together:

AG BALANCE SHEET

A	L
(I have . . .)	(I owe . . .)
Apartment	thirty-five years
Car	
Furniture	
$3,100 in the Bk	
$450 under the mattress	
Parking space	

In other words, what they'd told him was the mortgage of his life now turned out to be a mortgage *on* his life. AG had sold his entire stock of T. He was, in fact, a T seller, just like so many other average guys. His heart sank. He'd been putting off the Rd-Hded Trmtes, expecting that their day would come, and now he saw with crystalline clarity that he'd never have T for them, and the mysteries of their reproductive system would forever haunt him like some unresolved matter, a duty he'd never fulfilled, which, at the final moment, upon death's door, would put him in the red, in suspension of payments, in absolute bankruptcy.

He said to himself that this wasn't right. Specifically, he said,

"This isn't right."

How could he have gotten himself so thoroughly up to his neck in debt, he who was a specialist in accounting? Was it the system's fault? AG drew up the balance sheet for the system, to see if that might cast some light on the matter.

"The system owns almost all my T, but it owes me nothing," AG said to himself. The figures were easy to show:

SYSTEM BALANCE SHEET

A	L
(Has . . .)	(Owes me . . .)
All my T	Nothing

Upon his discovery, his heart sank even further—cold sweat, uncontrollable urges to kill his brother-in-law, the curtain guy, his father-in-law, the Bk manager, his boss and his wife, his natural sciences teacher. . . . He must awaken AGW. He ran into the bedroom.

"Honey! Honey, wake up!"

His wife gave a start.

"My God! What's wrong?"

"AGW, my love, I won't be able to devote my life to watching Rd-Hded Trmtes reproduce till I'm seventy-five years old!"

His wife rubbed her eyes.

"It's four in the morning! Are you out of your mind?"

"No, no! It's the *world* that's out of *its* mind! Thirty-five years of hiding bills, every day, from Monday to Friday! And all for what? Love of my life, we have to do something. I've spent too much T away from my true calling, Trmtes."

AGW sent her husband off to sleep on the sofa, despite the fact that it had just been reupholstered. She decided that the next day she'd take him to a shrink with a fake diploma recommended by some neighbor. I say neighbor, because I don't know anyone who doesn't say they have a neighbor who's nuts.

The neighbor in question turned out to be the woman from 4B, who had recently fallen in love with her psychologist, who was ostensibly helping her to improve her communication skills with her kids. Nothing extraordinary about that except for the fact that she hadn't had any kids yet. "One mustn't leave things for another day," she said. Her husband had tried to dissuade her, but she, who might best be described as bullheaded, embarked on a therapy that consisted of interpreting drawings by the children of other patients. Of course, the neighbor could hardly bring her own, nor were they going to analyze the doctor's drawings.

The psychologist was an Argentinean of Russian origin: Doctor Nicolás Tcherenolojov, but we shall call him Dr. Che, which is shorter.

To put it briefly, in our brief form, it so happened that AGW convinced AG to go see Dr. Che about the Rd-Hded Trmtes.

But our hero was reluctant to place his trust in Dr. Che. To begin with, AG suspected that Dr. Che was no doctor, not even Russian, and, most likely, not Argentinean either. After AGW had given a full account of her concerns, Dr. Che turned to AG.

"Look, you won't be able to devote your life to observing the reproductive system of the Rd-Hded Trmte until you have enough $. And you'll never have a healthy savings account unless you have your own business; but, let's admit it, you haven't the foggiest idea of how to start a business, and so you should sign up for a course in business for beginners. However, you don't have T for that, for the sole reason that you spend so many of your waking hours at IBN. Therefore, you should sign up for one of those home-schooling courses in weekly installments. Personally, I recommend the course by World Professionals. They're excellent!"

AGW was stunned. She sent her husband out to the waiting room next door.

"Are you out of your mind?" she screamed at Dr. Che.

"Calm down, calm down, madam!"

"What do you mean, calm down? As if we didn't already have enough problems with the Rd-Hded Trmtes."

Dr. Che took a deep breath, waited for AGW's temper to cool, and spoke with an air of authority.

"Hear me out. Your husband suffers from obsessive hysteria. And obsessions cannot be dealt with head-on, because all that that accomplishes is an aggravation of the obsession. In your husband's case, the obsession has taken the form of the Rd-Hded Trmte. Most likely we are dealing with some unresolved matter from his childhood, something that only conventional psychoanalysis could reveal, but that would take a long T, and by then you and your husband would be utterly destitute. No, we must undertake a strategic therapy, which would consist of deliberately introducing an element of distraction in order to gradually diminish the importance of the object of the obsession. In this case, I have chosen the course by installments using whatever pretext, like starting a business. I might have chosen a collection of Senegalese stamps, fifteenth-century monocles, or chopsticks, but I decided on the business-for-beginners course because he should see some logic in the suggestion. Otherwise your husband wouldn't have taken the bait. And he took it, all right. Did you see? He's absolutely convinced about taking the course!"

"And?" AGW asked.

"And he'll never finish it," Dr. Che proclaimed triumphantly as he swiveled in his chair. "No one ever finishes all the lessons in those courses. So, home-schooling by installments is the therapy that I use on all my patients who suffer obsessive hysteria like that of your husband. These courses have proved highly effective in eliminating all forms of obsessions, no matter how rare or persistent, because no human being ever finishes them. Shall I tell you what will happen? AG will start his business-for-beginners course, and without realizing it he'll forget about those horrid bugs. Then he'll get tired of the course, and he'll give that up too. And, soon, one fine day, he'll realize that he no longer cares about one thing or the other. Bye-bye Rd-Hded Trmtes and bye-bye home-schooling. Then, your husband will be completely sane."

They left the doctor's office. AG went directly to a newsstand to buy his first installment. AGW went to a bar to cry, and that day their life changed forever.

13

c2

AG Gets Ready

W hat never occurred to Dr. Che was that AG might indeed finish the course. As the partition between the good doctor's office and his waiting room was rather thin, AG had heard everything the doctor said to his wife, and so he now knew better than to mention the Rd-Hded Trmtes. Mum would be the word till AGW was convinced that the therapy had worked. Otherwise, she'd be on her guard and put two and two together when it came time to start his own business. He'd feign normality, give the impression of being well-adjusted, an obedient citizen willing to sell his own T to the system. No one must suspect that he was cunningly preparing to cross the point of no return.

So, in the presence of AGW, he spoke not a word about Trmtes and read his lessons. He studied diligently up to the tenth installment. And then, when he saw that the stage was set for the next act, he started leaving false clues to his expected loss of interest. Two weeks without studying business. Another week's installment cast deliberately on the sofa, apparently forgotten; three weeks later, another. And finally, no more installments around the home.

He never gave in to the temptation to study on the train, for fear of being spotted by a neighbor, who in turn might casually mention it to AGW. This severely restricted his field of action, leaving AG little T for his daily coursework. Once again, however, our hero acted wisely.

The bathroom is a place of true inspiration. Geniuses would never dare to admit it, but many of humankind's greatest ideas, many of the discoveries hit upon by illustrious scientists who changed the world or saved millions of lives, much of the most heavenly music ever composed, were conceived as the creator sat upon the throne.

And that's how it was. To avoid being found out, AG completed his studies in IBN's men's room. Seated there, with his trousers down around his ankles, in a less than dignified position, he soaked up everything an upstart entrepreneur needed to know about business. His father would have been proud to see him study like that. (For his devotion rather than his stance, I mean.)

But this period of discreet caution was about to come to an end; after months and months of study, AG had only one installment left to complete the course. It was then that he determined to devote his daily hour in the men's room to spawning ideas: he had to come up with an original product that would make him a millionaire. The course talked about a technique known as "brainstorming," which consisted in getting as many Post-it notes as you could find and filling them with all the ideas that a group of people could come up with. Then, you stuck the notes on the wall. He snuck off with roughly forty packs of Post-it notes and locked himself in the men's room. To fire his imagination, he put Wagner on the walkman, slipped on the headphones, picked up his pen, and started to think.

"All right, what do people need? Clearly, people want $. OK, I could sell $. No, that's out. It hardly makes sense to sell $. Though if I managed to get more than face value, it'd be a great business. . . . Yeah, but that's what Bks do already. I'll have to come up with something new and different. If I don't, I'll never be a millionaire."

Just in case, though, he put "$" on a Post-it note and stuck it on the wall. He continued.

"People need love. We're all short on cuddles and caresses. No. No, I can't sell love, that's what those clubs are for."

He jotted "love" on another bit of paper and stuck it up beside its predecessor. The truth is that he was having the T of his life: brainstorming felt great.

"Patience. People need to be more patient. No. Forget that. If I started telling people how to be more patient they'd only get irritated. Besides, you only have to try and get some official business done to see that bureaucrats are already the model of patience."

Nonetheless, he dutifully wrote "patience" and stuck it on the wall.

"People need to laugh. Nope. Out. Accountants don't know how to laugh. It'd be disaster. Besides, politicians already have a corner on the market. . . ."

But he noted down "laughter" and stuck it on the wall with the other ideas.

T flew by and he didn't realize that he had spent over three and a half hours sticking yellow slips of paper on the walls of the men's room stall. For a moment he thought he heard voices outside. But before he could return to his senses, to the final measures of *Tannhäuser,* the door came crashing down upon him and there stood an IBN security guard, the personnel director, and all his colleagues, including the department secretary.

Sitting in the men's room stall, pen in hand, two hundred Post-it notes stuck to the walls with words like "love," "laughter," "$," and "patience" written on them, AG found himself unable to articulate a convincing explanation that might justify the scene at the center of which he sat.

"What the H are you doing?" asked the personnel director.

"We've been looking for you all over for hours. It's time to go. Didn't you hear us calling you?" the secretary chimed in, indignant.

Out on the street, feeling as low as the ground, it occurred to him to go see his best friend, the only person he could trust with a secret, the only one who would keep it to himself: David, a plump, fifty-something baker and grocer, whose establishment was a few minutes from IBN.

"What brings you here?" David called when he saw AG walk through the door of his little store. AG didn't even bother to look up.

"Don't ask," he sighed.

"Bad day?"

"Horrible, David, it's been horrible. You wouldn't believe it. . . . I'd rather not talk about it. . . . Just tell me one thing. Is it tough being your own boss?"

David leaned on his broom and regarded AG a moment.

"Look, at your age don't go looking for trouble. Things aren't so good and you're in no position to stick your neck out. If you quit and your business doesn't do so good you'll have an H of a T finding another job. How many people in your neighborhood are out of work?" he said.

"About seventy percent, according to the census."

"Seven out of ten? You make the call."

That was not what AG wanted to hear. He had expected David to tell him, go on, you can do it, something like that. The sort of encouragement that doesn't really mean much, but that everyone who's about to go into business needs to hear to overcome the dizziness of the imminent leap into the entrepreneurial void. David's answer was sincere, if hardly gratifying.

"But, AG, if you finally decide to do it, you can always count on me. Whatever you need. You know you're my best friend," he added with a smile.

AG returned the smile. In fact, that was all he'd needed, a smile.

He headed home. What should he do now? After this afternoon's events, it would be rather hard to preserve his dignity at IBN. Everyone would be talking about him. How inconspicuously could he steal off to the toilet now? No. It was clear that the T had come to quit. He had to talk to AGW that very night. How would she take it?

The kids were more tired than usual and, after dining on a meatball and fifteen chocolate chip cookies each, getting tucked into bed, crying out for water nine times and going to the bathroom another six, they fell sound asleep.

"I want to start my own business," AG said abruptly to his wife.

Incredible. She didn't even bat an eye. How could she fail to make the connection with Dr. Che? Didn't she remember? Here was the proof that AG had executed his strategy masterfully. The only thing AGW asked him, before switching off the light, was if he'd need more $.

"No. Not a cent, yet."

"Well then, do as you please," she answered indifferently, as if she failed to see any problem.

As they settled down to sleep, it suddenly struck AG that he'd neglected to tell her about quitting his job at IBN—a minor detail he'd carelessly omitted. Oh well, what's done is done, and AG knew that when a couple had managed to agree on something, best leave well enough alone.

AG drifted off to sleep a very happy man, for he was about to go into business for himself. AGW also slept happily, thinking her husband was cured. And Dr. Che, too, slept contentedly, for the woman from 4B had moved in with him.

The next morning, since he was going to quit his job, AG left home quite a bit later than usual. He got on the train. In the last ten years not once had he found a seat, the train was always packed, with commuters pressed up against each other. But at this hour the train ran nearly empty. AG asked himself why they didn't hook these empty cars on to the back of the train at rush hour, but he couldn't come up with any reasonable answer. He sat down. Never having had the opportunity before, he didn't know how to position himself in the seat. He crossed his legs, he leaned back, he sat up, he stretched his legs out, he even curled up into the fetal position, but he could not find a comfortable position. The experience of actually *sitting* on a train was just too novel. After a minute or two, unable to stand it for another instant, he stood up. He clung to a bar and pressed his face against the window of the door, to the astonishment of two ladies who rode in the same car.

He rode the rest of way literally adhered to the glass, rehearsing the words he would put to his boss.

"I quit."

No, that would be too abrupt.

"I can't take it anymore."

No, that would denote weakness.

"I'm relinquishing my position."

A bit formal, perhaps.

"I'm offering my resignation."

What if they refused it?

Best to improvise. He finally arrived at his destination, exited the station, crossed the street and walked into IBN. His colleagues greeted him with nervous stares and averted eyes. What nerve, arriving so late to hide bills. But no one dared challenge him, for AG strode through like a gunslinger out of the old West, poised to draw the Colt .45

from his hip. With a slow, sure gait, he passed by his desk and headed directly for the boss's office. For the first time in his life he didn't knock at the door; he pushed it open with a firm shove and growled.

"I've decided to leave the firm."

But he got no answer. The office was empty. A voice came from behind him.

"He won't be back till next week. Would you like to leave a message?" said the boss's secretary without looking up, in the matter-of-fact tone of a bureaucrat answering the phone.

AG opted not to respond. He went directly to the seventh floor, to the personnel director's office. He too was out and no one knew where he was. He took the elevator up to the top floor, determined to see the general manager. The secretary told him he was out of town for a couple of weeks, at least. AG then asked for the president, but no one knew when he came into work. It was an outrage! There was no one to inform of his decision to quit. Finally, he handed a letter of resignation to the cleaning lady, who promised to make sure it got to one of the bosses.

Before abandoning the desk that had brought him so much unhappiness, he showed his colleagues where he had stashed all the bills they would have to find in the coming months, God forbid he should leave any unresolved business. AG didn't want to inconvenience anyone with his resignation.

He took the elevator down to the ground floor and exited the building. He felt an extraordinary sense of liberation. He started to run as fast as his legs would carry him. He didn't know where he was going. He just wanted to run and run some more. Every few steps, he leapt into the air, his arms raised as if he aimed to fly off, like a ballet dancer in a tutu. He felt lighter than air, joyful, free. His elation was such that he started turning cartwheels across the street. A cop stopped him and asked to see some ID, but, upon hearing that AG had just quit his job to start his own business, asked for his autograph instead.

After two hours of prancing around town, he went to the newsstand where he bought the weekly business course installments. The last one had arrived. He bid farewell to the news seller with an effusive hug. The fellow didn't quite understand the reason for such a warm good-bye, unaware that AG had always thought of him as the headmaster of his paper university. And in the Unnamed Settled Area all headmasters got a farewell hug.

He entered a café and sat at a little table. He started poring over the pages like a man possessed. He devoured that last installment, knowing that when he'd finished he'd finally be ready to join the ranks of the entrepreneurial.

Dr. Che had been right: no one ever finished a series of installments. Except AG! And so he was the only person in the Unnamed Settled Area who read the last sentence in the last installment, and, for that very reason, the only one who was going to get into the mess he was about to cause.

The last sentence read:

"In sum, a successful business
must develop products or services
that satisfy consumers' needs."

AG's mouth dropped open. He might have skipped the previous two hundred and seventy-six installments, for with that sentence, that simple sentence, he now knew everything he needed to know about business. All the reading he'd done so far now proved useless; this summary made it absolutely clear which product would make him the richest person on the planet. There it was, right under his nose! Satisfy needs! So that was it! Now he got it!

Leaving his coffee half drunk, he paid and rushed out to flag down a cab to Aaron's office. Aaron was the lawyer who had helped him with the mortgage ten years ago. He walked into the office.

"Aaron, I'm going into business. I need to get it going ASAP. We start now."

Aaron took paper and pen and began to take down all the relevant information.

"Name of the company?"

AG hesitated not an instant.

"Freedom, Inc."

"Business?"

"Satisfying the needs of man."

"Prostitution is illegal."

"No, no!" AG protested. "There's another, more ethical way to satisfy needs."

Aaron nodded.

"OK. 'Satisfying the needs of man.' Business address?"

AG gave him his home address, for he hardly had the $ to rent, much less buy, an office. After filling out a series of forms, the lawyer asked him for a retainer and assured him that he would send him all the necessary documentation forthwith.

Upon leaving the lawyer's office, AG realized he had a problem. The learn-by-installments course was quite specific on the point that, like the founders of Hewlett-Packard and so many other successful entrepreneurs, in order to triumph in business one had to set up shop in a garage. And AG didn't have a garage, just a parking space. He'd fix that. He phoned an office furnishing company and had them fit glass partitions, with Venetian blinds, on the three lines that separated his parking space from those of his neighbors. On the fourth side, originally intended to provide access for the user's car, he had a door put in.

It cost him just about everything he had in the Bk, but it was worth it. Freedom, Inc. was a reality and, like the book said, it was born in a garage.

Back home, that same day, he took the dining-room table, the entrance hall lamp, a kitchen chair and the kids' computer and moved them all down to the parking space, or rather his new headquarters. Truth be told, the kids' computer only served for videogames, but an office isn't an office without a computer screen on the desk, and his would be no exception.

He was exhausted, but happy.

Suddenly he heard a car outside. It was AGW, who had gone to pick up the kids from school. She shouted, red-faced.

"What's going on!? They've closed off our parking space! The Bk! It must be the Bk! I'll bet AG got behind on the payments!"

Her husband stuck his head out the door of his parking-space office and suggested a solution.

"Park in 4B's spot. She moved in with Dr. Che. Her space is empty."

The fact is that AG had all his bases covered. When AGW found out that their parking space was her husband's new office, she nearly fainted. But when AG told her he'd quit his job at IBN she really fainted.

"Why did you do it? Why?" she asked, her face still deathly pale.

"For the Trmtes, my love. I'm sorry," AG answered.

She broke down in tears. The children too. And when she heard over the phone, his mother-in-law did too. Then AGW called AG's sister, and they cried together. Listening on the other line, AG heard his brother-in-law guffaw in the background.

Then AGW called Dr. Che.

"Your grand plan turned out to be a disaster. Not only did AG finish the learn-by-installments course you prescribed him, he's still stuck on the damn Trmtes."

Dr. Che was silent. Then he spoke.

"Look, let's talk about this in my office. We need to interpret your children's drawings. Tomorrow bring me two improv drawings by each of them. You'll see how some interesting points come up. . . ."

AGW was livid.

"Look, I know what you're getting at! I saw how you looked at me with those lecherous eyes in your office. Let me tell you something: it's one thing to cure my husband, but it's quite another thing to cheat on my neighbor."

That made feel AG better.

They put the kids to bed. AGW had yet to say a word to her husband. She was furious. They got into their pajamas and into bed in silence. It was then that AG knew the time had come to share his discovery, the secret enclosed in the last sentence in business-for-beginners collection.

He switched on the lamp on the night table.

"What are you doing?" his wife asked, turning toward him.

AG donned the same enigmatic expression as when he'd presented her engagement ring. He put his hand in his pajama pocket and pulled out quite another thing: a little plastic vial. AGW recognized it immediately: it was the sort she used when she had to take a urine sample.

"What's that?"

"It's the chance of our lifetime. It's the product that's going to make us millionaires. Something nobody ever thought of before, because nobody ever had the perseverance that I had to get to installment number two hundred and seventy-eight."

"Urine?"

"No, listen: it's T. I put five minutes in this vial. Rule number 1 in business is that success means offering a product that satisfies a need. I've discovered the philosopher's stone of business. When I read that sentence, when I saw that business was all about satisfying needs, I saw the light. I only had to look at myself. I've sold forty years of my own T. What attracted me to the home-learning course was a need for T; nobody has it. And despite the fact that everybody wants it, nobody sells it. In this society, we've all sold our T to the system, we're all T sellers and we've lost control over our own lives. My invention will allow people to buy it back. Vials of five minutes. . . . Don't you see? We're practically millionaires already! Don't you think that's wonderful?"

AGW took the vial and opened it. It was empty. She was utterly bewildered. She was on the verge of a nervous breakdown, but she composed herself.

"AG, explain to me right now what this inane idea about putting five minutes in a urine bottle is all about. Don't tell me you quit your job for this. I've never heard anything so absurd in my life."

"Listen, listen! This is just another consumer product, like whatever they sell in the supermarket. Anyone can buy this bottle, he opens it and has five minutes of T for himself, he consumes them, and then throws the bottle away. Don't you think it's the greatest invention of the century?"

AGW still didn't get it. She despaired.

"Are you quite unaware that we have no $? On my salary, we can survive for two, maybe two and a half months. We'll be out on the street in no T. What will become of our children? We'll have to beg your brother-in-law for more $ and we still owe him for the lace curtains."

Reminded of the curtains, AGW again couldn't hold back the tears. She was inconsolable. Nonetheless, AG tried to console her.

"Sweetheart, it's the chance of our lifetime. Trust me. This product is going to make us rich. You don't know what I've learned. I used more than four hundred Post-it notes to get this far. I've read three hundred installments of business-for-beginners. I know more than you think."

AGW felt sorry. She knew that her husband was doing all this to make something of himself. It was not an act of egoism but of survival, but it was her duty to make him see that, from the point of view of the family econ-omy, his decision was suicide. The thought softened her heart. She composed herself and looked him in the eye.

"One week. I'll give you one week. If you don't make it, I'm going back to my parents. It's up to you."

She rolled over and turned out the light. That was enough for AG. AGW had acquiesced, and he had a week to get his business off the ground. It would be tough—but not impossible. And something told him that, despite being an AG, he could do it.

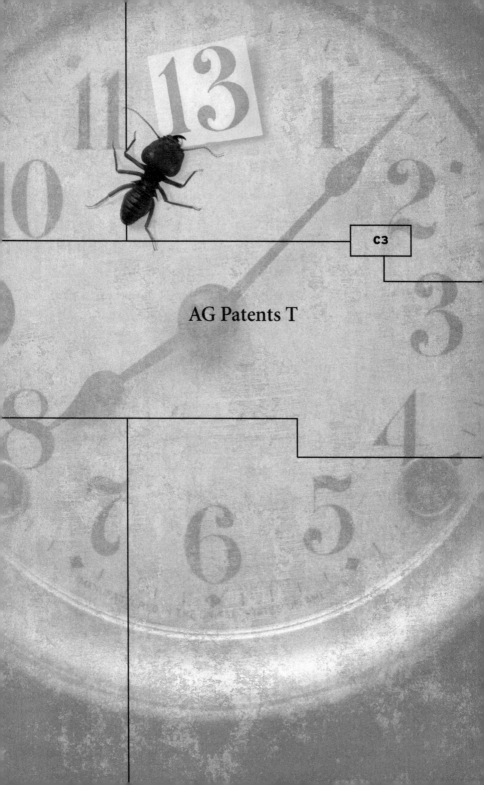

At six in the morning AG was already up and about. Five working days and a million things to do. He went down to his office (his parking space, that is). Working in the parking space had one slight problem: light. There were no plugs, which rendered the entrance hall lamp mere decoration, and he had to work by the main lights of the garage. But, as most garage lights do, they went off automatically every few minutes. This caused great inconvenience—every few minutes he had to trudge over to the exit and switch them back on.

He spent the morning drawing up a list of steps to take over the next five days. When he'd finished, he went upstairs to his apartment. The phone rang. It was the head of Human Resources! When AG told him he'd left the company for the Rd-Hded Trmte, the HR-Drctor made a surprising confession.

"It's strange. I didn't know we had so much in common. I understand your decision perfectly. What's more, I deeply admire you. I've been waiting for years to retire to devote myself to the brown-nosed beetle. I find it fascinating how they kick up their heels and stick their head in the mud. . . . No, no! I'm not insinuating that the Rd-Hded Trmte is less interesting, but the brown-nosed beetle . . ."

They had a fine T sharing their discoveries regarding insects.

"I hope that some day both our dreams come true," the HR-Drctor said finally.

After he'd hung up, AG set off for the station and caught a city-bound train. He spent the whole trip pasted to the door contemplating his vialful of five minutes. He admired it through the light, held high, like a precious stone, like a diamond in the rough. His fellow passengers could barely contain their disgust. AG was the only one who saw T. The others saw a urine bottle, which, although empty, was impossible to imagine without the yellow fluid inside.

The train pulled in. He went to the Central Office of Patents and Trademarks. There were but a few people in the patents line: most people think everything's already been invented. After a few minutes it was his turn.

"Well, and what is it you want to patent?" the civil servant asked.

AG showed him his vial of T.

"This."

The civil servant snatched the urine bottle from his hands and examined it. Then he returned it.

"That cannot be patented," he spat. "There's been a patent on urine sample bottles for years. Application denied. Next!"

"Wait, wait! It's not what you think. It's not the bottle. It's what's inside."

He beckoned him to come close and whispered in his ear.

"There's five minutes in this bottle. Look, look. . . . Can't you see them?"

The civil servant's reaction hardly differed from AGW's the day before.

"Are you telling me you want to patent five minutes of T?!" he bawled.

"Ssshhhhh! Not so loud, for the love of God, this is strictly on the QT. No, no. I'm not trying to patent five minutes of T. My patent is for bottling them. Read my application." He handed him the form. "It says clearly: *packaged minutes.*"

The civil servant sighed. He typed something into his computer, waited and turned back to AG.

"Look, let me explain how this patent thing works. You can patent whatever you want as long as it hasn't been patented before. I've searched the archives and, indeed, there is no patent on such a stu—such an idea. I'll stamp your application, send it to the registry and that's that. But your selling it is another thing altogether. It's like if you patent a flying submarine. I'll patent it if you want, but if it doesn't fly, I can assure you it won't get you anywhere. Do you understand?"

"Perfectly." AG could hardly contain his joy.

"OK, then take this form to the Trade Office and ask for a Sales Permit. But I'm telling you they won't give you one. Because this is the weirdest thing I've seen in years, and I can assure you that I've seen some very, very weird things."

AG thanked him. The patent on bottled-saleable-T was his exclusively. He went across town to the Trade Office. He slipped in just as they were closing the doors.

He got in line, his urine bottle in hand. Finally, his turn came.

"I want to apply for a permit to sell this product," and he held up the bottle.

The civil servant glanced at him and, to his surprise, answered, "No problem. You can market that."

AG couldn't believe it: it was the first time someone had understood him.

"Really?" he asked.

"Of course!" exclaimed the civil servant. "It's a urine bottle. Urine sample bottles are authorized in this country. You can sell urine bottles, but I warn you, the competition is ferocious, eh?"

"No, no!" AG corrected him. "Look closer, it's a bottle of five minutes. It says so right on the label. See? Five minutes."

The civil servant stared in amazement.

"You're telling me you want to sell bottles of five minutes?"

AG nodded.

"That's right. What's wrong with that?"

The civil servant was flustered.

"Look, I've never had to deal with anything like this. My job is to check that any product to be sold is safe, environmentally friendly, that it meets quality standards, that the contents comply with Health Department specifications. . . . But five minutes? That I've never seen before. I'm sorry, but I'll have to call my supervisor."

The aforesaid supervisor, a rather sour-faced man, came out of a nearby office and listened attentively to the civil servant, after which he took no more than a second to respond.

"No. You cannot sell this. You cannot sell T. Your application is denied."

AG could hardly believe his ears. He had the patent on the idea of the century and this lamebrain wouldn't let him sell it. Suddenly, he saw his brother-in-law doubled over with laughter, while AGW, with children and suitcases, headed out the door for her parents' place.

With renewed energy, he shouted, "Listen to me! They sell pills to stop people having kids, they sell parachute jumps, they sell stag parties. . . ." Now he was truly hysterical. "Don't you realize that you are committing an outrage against society and the freedom to consume?! If someone wants to buy T, they have every right to do so. It's their $! They pay for it, they consume it, and they throw away the bottle. Just like a bag of potato chips! If you don't give me a permit to sell T, I'll report you for obstructing the system, the free society we've created, which is based on trade. You are committing an outrage against the market economy!"

AG was beside himself; by the end of his diatribe his voice had risen to a scream. The supervisor took the civil servant aside.

"Look, the big B, the Trade Office Director, plans to run for a seat on the city council. The election's coming up and things don't look good. He's in the middle of the campaign and he told me explicitly that he does not want any problems right now. If this moron denounces us and it comes out in the papers, his political career will be over before it got started. And that means problems for us too. This guy is totally wacko, just look at him. Give him the authorization. After all, he's not going to sell a single bottle of the stuff. And, besides, there's a game on TV and if we don't get out of here we're going to miss it. But think up something to sort of hamstring him. Some sort of catch, I don't know, anything to put a leash on him. He's a sap."

The supervisor turned and disappeared back into his office. The civil servant returned to his post and addressed AG.

"All right. We'll grant you the authorization to sell your product. But . . . there's one thing . . . yes, you must guarantee the customer that each bottle actually contains five minutes of T. Otherwise, it's fraud. You'd be selling air. Therefore, you cannot sell or attempt to sell any bottle that has not been open for five minutes, timed with a clock. Only then will we consider that the bottle contains T and that it meets the quality standards for sale. Is that clear?"

"Certainly," AG replied. "What did you think, that I was going to sell empty vials?"

The civil servant stamped the seal on the official application form. AG was now authorized to sell T to the good citizens of the Unnamed Settled Area.

He spent the following day in his parking space, putting the final touches on his project to market bottled T. The truth was that the choice of the urine bottle had been something of an error. This he had seen with his own eyes. In light of his experience with the civil servants the previous day, how would the public react when they saw them on the supermarket shelf? No one would know that they contained T, and that would put a damper on his sales. Even in the hypothetical case that they knew that the vials contained T, people might assume that the five minutes were exclusively for relieving themselves. But no, the five minutes were for whatever the buyer desired. It was essential that the contents of the bottle be absolutely clear.

To lend a touch of class, many products are marketed with a name that includes the maker, which serves as a sort of guarantee. For instance, "Levi's 501 Jeans" or "Acqua di Gió by Giorgio Armani," according to the desired tone. In his case, it was clear. The product was five minutes and his company was called Freedom, Inc. He settled on *Five Minutes of Freedom.*

Now that he had a catchy name, he needed a logo. He was tempted to design it himself. He remembered, however, that in the learn-by-installments course they recommended delegating design tasks to an expert. So he went upstairs and asked AG-1 to draw a logo. No one could have done it better.

He returned to his parking space. There was another crucial decision that AG had to face: how much should he charge for five minutes of T?

The question went beyond commercial considerations and into the realm of the philosophical, and thus the unanswerable. How much were five minutes of a person's life worth? He tried to visualize what would happen. John Q. Customer walks into a supermarket and spots a bottle of five minutes on the shelf. He buys it. That same day, at the office, he consumes his five minutes, thus leaving his work unfinished. His B goes mental but has no choice but to put up and shut up, since the consumption of T is authorized by the State, as anyone could see from the permits AG now had in his possession. True, from the legal point of view, the consumption of T conflicted with other obligations, such as, for example, the workday or the provision of certain services. These sorts of contradictions, however, were nothing new in the Unnamed Settled Area: they also made cars that went a hundred and fifty miles an hour when the limit was seventy-five; they allowed certain industrial activities associated with levels of pollution which exceeded those agreed at international environmental forums; they sold tobacco despite the fact that it caused fatal illnesses. Thus it was clear: sell—at all costs, without a care for the consequences. Selling T would conflict with certain activities, that was clear; but so long as consumption was being created, it would trump all competitors. Consumption was the highest-ranking business in the country. It created growth.

His thoughts returned to the price to put on the five minutes. Ideally, each person would pay an amount equal to what they earned for five minutes of work. Why? Well, in a certain way that would be their opportunity cost. Problem: each person earns a different salary. A street sweeper earns less than an office clerk, who earns less than a financial director, who earns less than a doctor, who earns less than a plumber, who earns less than a builder, who earns more than everyone. But pricing each bottle according to the buyer was not an option; it would hardly be equitable because five minutes of an individual's T are five minutes of a life, and people's lives are worth the same, regardless of sex, race, religion, or social class.

What to do? It was clear as day. He'd have to take a chance. If it worked, people of all income brackets would buy vials of T. From the biggest earners to the smallest. But, like everything in life, it would all come down to an average: the average salary for the country.

Therefore, the next step would be to calculate how much was paid in the Unnamed Settled Area for five minutes of a citizen's T, on average. That was easy: all he had to do was to calculate what they paid him for five minutes out of a workday. After all, AG was an average citizen with an average salary. Whenever he went to ask for a raise, the HR-Drctor told him he had no right to any such thing.

"Forget it. The accountant's profession is average for professionals. The salaries in our sector are average for all industrial sectors. And our company pay is pegged at the sector average. You are the average of the average of the average. Besides AG, you don't want to be above average, people don't like that."

So he calculated his earnings for five minutes of work at IBN. When he saw the figure, he was stunned: had he known before, he wouldn't have waited so long to quit his job. Society valued five minutes of his T at seventeen cents.

To that amount he added tax and markup and arrived at the neat sum of forty cents. He reflected a moment on that amount and decided that if they charged eighty cents for five units of chewing gum, a vial of five minutes ought to be worth a good deal more. He raised the price from forty cents to $1.99. He contemplated that price, retraced the process he'd followed and suddenly was assailed by a feeling of profound disappointment, for his price-setting method had now lost all sheen of professionalism. What AG didn't know was that he had calculated the price exactly the way the vast majority of businesses do.

AG realized he was tired, so he decided to go out for a cigarette, despite the fact that he neither smoked nor had any cigarettes. But when people who smoke say they're going out for some fresh air, they light up. . . .

Once outside, he recalled what the civil servant from the Trade Office had told him. He was obliged to put a clock by each bottle for five minutes, in order to verify the contents. AG had only an alarm clock. With a single alarm clock he could fill barely two hundred vials a day, and at that rate he'd never be a millionaire. The only thing to do was to fill several vials simultaneously with several alarm clocks.

Back in his hutch, he added the purchase of dozens of alarm clocks, in addition to vials, to his list of chores for the next day.

It was late. He went upstairs for supper. As he was about to head back down to work, AGW made him put on his pajamas, saying that when he came back from the office so late, he woke her up. He was horrified, for there wasn't a night, then or thereafter, on which one of his neighbors coming home from the movies or an evening out on the town didn't see him working in his robe in his cubicle. "Working overtime, eh?" they'd quip.

Thus dressed, he spent the rest of the night doing endless calculations of how many alarm clocks and vials he would need. Then he took another few hours trying to think up an advertising slogan. He made a short list of possibilities, and then discarded them one by one, unconvinced.

"This T is fantastic."

"Good quality T."

"There's no T to lose."

"Free T cheap."

"The T we live in."

"T out."

"Special: Five minutes for $1.99."

He was exhausted. His whole body ached. He'd had to get up two hundred times to switch on the garage lights. He gave up; it was a quarter to five in the morning. He'd give it more thought the next day. He'd have to get up at seven to pick up all the material on the list. He didn't turn off the office light, it switched itself off, and he took the elevator up. He crept in the door and into the bedroom. Having forgotten that he was already dressed for his next endeavor, he shed his pajamas, cursed silently and put them back on.

When he slipped into bed, AGW stirred and, from the depths of slumber, mumbled, "Did you make a sale yet?"

"No, not yet."

"Well, hurry up, T's running out."

AG bolted upright, he leapt from the bed and cried out, startling his wife from her sleep.

"Eureka! That's it! You got the slogan! *Hurry up, T's running out!*"

AG fell back on his pillow and slept. AGW, on the other hand, didn't sleep a wink for the rest of the morning. Her husband's condition was clearly getting worse.

AG Produces T

T
he next morning, despite having slept only two hours, AG awoke with admirable spunk. He insisted on driving AGW to work and the kids to school, for today he needed the car. He drove around town until he found a large enough clock shop. He bought twenty alarm clocks, which he put in the trunk of his car. He could have made do with fewer alarm clocks, it's true, but something might go wrong during the filling process. Most everyone knows that bottling lines break down every once in a while, and there was no reason his should be an exception.

He then sped over to Vials & Vials, a packaging man-ufacturer he'd found the preceding day in the yellow pages.

"And what do you want these two thousand vials for?" queried an engineer as they sat face-to-face in the customers' meeting room. "I need to know so we can choose a model that will hold precisely the volume you want to put in it," he said by way of clarification.

"Well, that's a good question. I have no idea what size I need," AG answered.

"Pardon!?"

"Well, you see . . . they're to hold five minutes of T."

The engineer was perplexed.

"I've never run into this sort of thing before. Such an order would entail extraordinary technical complexity. I'll have to inform the chief engineers from each of our technical departments."

AG was growing impatient, T was short. He tried to dissuade him.

"No, really. It doesn't matter. After all, I only need a container that will hold five minutes—"

But the engineer interrupted him, offended.

"What do you mean, it doesn't matter? Do you realize what you are saying? At Vials & Vials we have never failed to provide the exact size. *'Not a milliliter more, not a milliliter less.'* That is our slogan."

The engineer disappeared as AG sat there helplessly, and a moment later there appeared four more men in white coats with insignia on the lapel that identified them as fellow engineers from the Vials & Vials Technical Board. The situation was getting more difficult; instead of just one engineer, he now had to contend with five.

"This customer has requested the ideal size for a vial to hold five minutes of T. Gentlemen, I await your suggestions on how to perform such a calculation."

Following a moment's reflection, one by one the engineers pulled notebooks out of their coat pockets and started scribbling formulas. AG couldn't believe his eyes. It was all much simpler than that: why did engineers insist on complicating things so? After an interminable quarter of an hour, the most white-haired engineer held up his hand, cleared his throat, and spoke.

"I have it. A minute of T is equivalent to sixty seconds. A second of wind at an average speed of eight point seven five miles per hour is equivalent to a half a cubic centimeter of air. Therefore, my estimate is that this gentleman needs vials measuring . . . one moment . . . yes, ninety cubic centimeters."

"I must disagree, sir," the director of the Quality Assessment Department cut in. "Your formula demonstrates astonishing simplicity. The problem is far more complex. T is a dimension relative to space. When Albert Einstein developed his General Theory of Relativity he showed that space cannot be separated from T. Therefore, the fundamental question in the choice of the vial that this gentleman requires is: at what speed will the T be bottled?"

All present turned and stared at AG to await his answer. He didn't know what to say. Finally, he spoke.

"Well . . . well . . . at the speed of . . . of . . . of T!"

The Vials & Vials engineers were dumbstruck. The youngest engineer raised his hand to speak.

"Thus, we are faced with an intractable problem! A reference system within another reference system. Bearing in mind that $E = mc^2$, the energy to be stored in the bottle can only be contained if we employ an ultra high-strength material capable of withstanding the pressure of the contents. That leads to another problem, because we cannot determine a suitable material for the container until we know how much space five minutes will occupy. We are stuck in a vicious circle. There is no solution!"

The discussion grew heated and the temperature in the meeting room rose ever higher. Another of the engineers, who had theretofore remained silent, intervened vehemently.

"So, what we are debating here is a matter of occupational safety! Depending on the speed at which this gentleman bottles his T, and the speed of deceleration in the bottling process, this could produce an increase in mass similar to that produced in nuclear power plants in the process of deceleration of the nucleus of an atom. It is crucial that this gentleman's production facilities remain free of uranium, at the risk of a major explosion! Have you considered that possibility, sir? Sir?"

But AG was no longer present. He'd left the room without the engineers from Vials & Vials ever noticing, and was now driving along in search of a pharmacy where he might buy standard urine sample bottles. He'd get his business done sooner. But, as he couldn't find the quantity he needed in any one establishment, he had to drive all over town from one druggist to the next until he'd acquired one thousand five hundred bottles.

With the purchase of a piece of white canvas for a sign and a laser printer for stick-on labels from a discount store, he wound up his errands.

AG was exhausted when he arrived back at his cage, but was able to muster the energy to continue working without rest. First he printed out one thousand five hundred stick-on labels with the following text:

> **This vial contains five minutes of time for your use and enjoyment. As soon as you open the bottle, the five minutes will be yours. Enjoy them!**

That made everything clear.

Then AG turned to the filling of his one thousand five hundred vials.

He arranged his twenty alarm clocks on the floor, one next to the other, in two rows of ten alarm clocks. At the head of each row, he placed a cardboard box containing the empty plastic vials, and at the other end he placed another box, into which he planned to deposit the full vials as the bottling process progressed.

He stood in front of the first alarm clock, took a urine vial and uncapped it. He took the alarm clock and set it to ring in five minutes. He did the same with the second vial and the second alarm clock, and then with the third, and with the fourth, and so on. When he got to the twentieth alarm clock the garage lights went out. He ran to switch them back on. He could see two rows of ten alarm clocks each, each clock with a urine vial in front of it. What a wonderful site his production line made! How exciting! He was actually bottling T! As he walked back from turning on the lights, the first alarm clock rang. A few seconds later the next one was already ringing.

Unnerved, AG ran to the first alarm clock, grabbed the vial lying in front of it, capped it, slapped on a stick-on label with his logo and instructions for use and put it in the box.

AG started to panic, the alarm clocks were ringing too long before he could shut them off. It wasn't that he was afraid of bothering his neighbors at this time of day, rather that he was overfilling the bottles. The first hundred vials must have gotten six or seven minutes extra. What a disaster! If he went on like this he'd end up losing money! He was producing vials with fifty percent extra free, like one of those special shampoo offers. It then came to him, the true significance of alarm.

Bit by bit he managed to get into the groove of the filling process. Open the bottle, set one alarm, shut off the next, cap the vial, slap on the label, run over to turn the light on, put the vial in the finished-product box, open another vial, set another alarm, and so on for hours until he had succeeded in filling the one thousand five hundred bottles.

AG was proud of himself. His first run had been a success. True, some of the bottles had been overfilled with T, and others were not well capped. In his comings and goings in the dark between the production lines a few bottles had tipped over, whose minutes only AG witnessed spilling out across the floor. He refilled them. He was fairly sure that no vial remained empty. It was essential to guarantee the customer quality.

It was late. AG would have to find somewhere to store the bottled T; if he left it in the parking space any unscrupulous character might steal it. Imagine what someone could do with so many free minutes!

Since AG had no storage space, he jimmied the door on the one allotted to 4B—after all, the owner had gone off to live with Dr. Che. He dumped 4B's few remaining possessions into a garbage bin across the street and stashed his one thousand five hundred vials full of T in the storage space.

AG was exhausted and in dire need of a shower. Of the last forty-eight hours he'd slept only two. Tomorrow would be a tough day. He had to start selling, the deadline his wife had given him to start earning $ was drawing near. Indeed, he had only two days left.

On the Ns

A G awoke still quite tired, but there was no T to rest. He grabbed his briefcase with the catalogue of prices, a single sheet on which he'd written:

Freedom, Inc
Ref. 0000000000000000000000000000000000001
Five minutes of freedom: $1.49
Distributor's margin: $0.50
Retail price: $1.99

AG loaded the one thousand five hundred vials into the trunk of his car, taking extreme care for fear they might explode. His awareness of the potential explosive properties of his vials, according to the theories of the engineers from Vials & Vials, obliged him to take certain precautions. Then he drove downtown. His first visit was to a café.

AG felt sure of himself, thinking only of the huge order they'd make when he showed them what he called the "invention of the century." After a fifteen-minute wait, he managed to get a moment with the manager. He took a deep breath, put on all the salesman's charm that an accountant could muster and blurted out,

"This is your lucky day. I'm here to offer you a once-in-a-lifetime chance. Your café is going to be the first establishment in town to sell this incredibly hot item."

AG proudly showed the manager a five-minute vial, filled to the brim, and smiled ear to ear. The café manager looked at him for a moment, then with spoke with disdain.

"Sorry. We don't sell urine here."

The smile melted from AG's face. He fumbled for words.

"No, no. I don't want to sell urine. This vial is from a pharmacy, but the important thing isn't what it's designed for, it's what's in it: Here inside are five minutes of T!" he said, regaining his initial élan and overcoming the impact of the first no.

"What was that you said?" the manager of the café asked, incredulous.

"Yes, yes. You heard right. I have a patent on the product and authorization from the Trade Office to sell vials of five minutes. Buy one and you got five minutes of T for yourself! You sell it at $1.99 and I sell it to you for $1.49. For every five minutes you sell, you get fifty cents. Not bad, eh?"

The manager of the café thought for a moment.

"Well, you see, what we want here is for the customer to sit down, order a cup of coffee or whatever, and get out of here ASAP—leaving his seat free for the next customer. If I sold bottles of five minutes in my café, my customers would stay longer before going back to work. That would mean less coffee and thus less trade. I agree that the product is rather novel, but for an establishment like mine to sell T would be a problem, because we'd sell less coffee, snacks, and refreshments. And that's what we live on, I regret to say."

AG left the café in a daze. He had expected enthusiasm and he got the door. But he composed himself. Maybe he'd just have to cross the entire catering sector off his list of potential customers. The best thing would be to forget about cafés and head straight for the big-box mart: a store that sold everything couldn't turn him down.

A hard-looking character waited on him. After seeing the product and checking the price, he asked AG to open it. Though he knew that he'd have to hand out samples to his potential customers if he wanted to get orders, AG wasn't thrilled about having to waste a bottle. The potential buyer opened the vial and peered inside.

"The packaging is great, and I don't see any manufacturing defects in the product."

AG smiled with satisfaction.

"However," he continued, "I'm sure you know our store slogan: *If you're not satisfied, your money back.* That means we accept all returns. Our slogan only allows us to sell products that the customer can return, so we can return their $. Your product doesn't meet that standard. If we sell bottles of five minutes and customers bring them back unhappy with the quality and the contents of their five minutes of T, what are we going to do? We can't recover the lost T. I understand you can bring me more bottles, but they won't be the same five minutes. The T consumed is lost forever, and we can't accept a nonreturnable product. That's against company policy and values, I'm afraid."

AG returned to his car, somewhat more worried. That was the second place that had showed no interest in his bottles of five minutes. Didn't they see what they had in their hands? AG drew a line through "Big-Box Marts" on his list of potential customers. He'd spent the whole morning on two leads and had nothing to show for it. He felt frustrated and downhearted. His world of customers had begun to shrink and he was running out of T to start earning $.

He skipped lunch, as he had no appetite. He was nervous and the image of the Rd-Hded Trmtes began to blur in his mind's eye. In the early afternoon he went to a gourmet carryout place.

"Look, you won't sell this product in carryout establishments. People want carryout food because they don't have the T to cook. It would be a disaster if people had the T to cook their own meals. Can you imagine? What a catastrophe! That would be our undoing! Sales would dry up in no T. I'm very sorry. Selling T is against our interests," the owner said when AG showed him his five-minute vials.

AG was no longer taken by surprise. He crossed gourmet carryouts off his list. What else could he do? Perhaps the problem lay in his dependence on retailers. Maybe the trick was to sell directly to the public, avoiding the retailers' conflicts of interest. Place his wares in public areas, busy spots where people would discover his bottles of T directly. He made several calls to the Town Council before finally getting through to the person in charge of vending machines at Public Transport. He set up an appointment for later that day. But then his potential buyer made a rather offhand remark.

"Look, the reason people take the metro is because it's fast. People don't have T to get around. If we sell bottles of five minutes, people will most likely use the T to walk and then they won't take the metro. I can't sell T in my stations, we'd lose passengers. You understand . . ."

What AG understood was that selling T was a threat to the system, a danger to all other products, a risk for any business. The lack of T was at the root of people's countless stress-producing needs. Selling T was a menace to consumer society.

Glumly, he spent the rest of the afternoon visiting an odd assortment of establishments, where, one after the other, they turned down his offer of five-minute vials.

He could think of nothing else to do. It was six in the evening on the day before the deadline AGW had given him and he had yet to earn a cent. He was sad and desperate. All his efforts had been in vain. He'd look for another job. He'd find another IBN and return to his previous nonlife.

He went back to his car. There was just one last chance: David, his best buddy. Of course, he couldn't force him to buy vials of T, but he could ask him to display them in his store. He took a U-turn at the next light. David smiled when he saw him; he hadn't heard from his friend for days. AG recounted all the events of the past days and showed him his five-minute vials.

"What a brilliant idea! My customers never stop complaining about how they don't have any T. Give me all your bottles, I'll put them here and we'll hang your sign in the window. Don't worry! You bet we'll sell some," David exclaimed enthusiastically.

But AG had lost all faith in his product. Nonetheless, he unloaded his one thousand five hundred bottles of five minutes and he stacked them up in a pyramid in David's grocery, by the door. Together they strung up the sign with the slogan that AGW had struck upon: *Hurry up, T's running out.* AG read his pitch once again and realized that, truly, his T had already run out. Irony of ironies! He felt like crying, but held back his tears for want of a handkerchief. He went home. He wanted to avoid AGW, fearing the sermon he would have to suffer. He knew that the next day he'd have to start looking for a job, so he went to bed at eight, before his mother-in-law came back with the kids. He fell asleep thinking sadly about the Rd-Hded Trmtes to which he could never dedicate his life.

When AGW got home and saw her husband sleeping she realized that things had gone as expected. Who else but her husband would think of selling T? Despite considering him a complete fool, she didn't awaken him, because she loved him. Clearly he was beat, sleeping there like a log. She felt sorry for him, and kissed him on the cheek. She put the kids to bed and had dinner alone while she scanned the want ads for a job for AG. She didn't turn on the TV so as not to disturb anyone. Thus she missed the news that night. The anchor was about say good night.

"And that's the weather. And now our strange news of the day. . . . Let's go downtown, where our city correspondent is standing by."

A peppy reporter stood by a pyramid of empty plastic vials, piled up next to a wall, holding a mike.

"A store here is offering a rather curious product," he said, as the camera zoomed in on the urine vial in his hand. "This is five minutes of conveniently packaged T, which anyone can buy for the price of $1.99. The purchase of this bottle gives you the right to five minutes for yourself. Yes, you heard me. Here, in this store, T is sold. Buy a bottle and you can take a break from work for that errand you never had T for, go have a cigarette at the bar down the street, go for a short stroll, pay a visit to that lover you haven't seen in a while . . . whatever you want to do. Because this product consists of five minutes—packaged in a vial! Standing right next to me is the owner of this establishment, which is the only place, so far, where these vials are sold."

The camera pulled back and David appeared on the screen, paunchy in his apron, a smile on his face.

"Can you tell us how this product works?" the reporter asked.

David outdid himself.

"Sure. You buy a bottle in my store, you open it and you get five minutes of T for *you*. Naturally, you can consume your five minutes whenever you please. Remember: the five minutes are yours and nobody else's. It's T that you didn't have, so, if you buy them, these minutes will be yours, it doesn't matter one bit where you are or what you're doing. Buy one, it's a real treat. By the way, can I say 'hi' to someone?"

This seemed to annoy the reporter.

David then ripped the mike out his hands. The camera zoomed in.

"AG, I hope you're watching this. I thought it might help. You studied lots about business, but you forgot the most important thing: TV. My store's right next door to the LocuVision studios, so I told the evening anchor-guy, the one who just introduced us. They loved it and they sent this guy over to interview me."

Now it was the reporter who snatched the microphone away from David. The camera swung back on to him and then the unexpected happened, the best advertising possible—proof.

Apparently the reporter was sick and tired of long hours.

"This product is registered with and authorized by the Trade Office and is intended to protect a right that no citizen of a free country can be deprived of. So, my cameraman, my broadcast technician, and I have just bought a vial of five minutes each, and we are going to try it right here and now."

He was joined on the screen by two other men: the cameraman, who had apparently left his camera on a tripod to continue filming, and the broadcast technician. Each held up a vial. Together they uncapped their vials.

"Please excuse us while we keep you here for another five minutes. We are all going to consume five minutes of freedom. Tonight's news will last five minutes longer than usual. I leave you with this shot of the store. We'll be right back."

Indeed, the camera stayed on the pile of urine bottles, with the sign and its slogan, *"Hurry up, T's running out."* Like a rather novel emergency test pattern, the scene remained unchanged for five minutes, no more, no less. A fair number of viewers watching the news that night started banging on their sets, thinking that maybe the picture had frozen due to a loose connection.

As soon as those five minutes were up, the reporter, having gone off to eat a piece of chocolate cake, reappeared. Millions of TV viewers had had to wait five minutes while the reporter ate his dessert before continuing with the program. No one could believe it. Here was the proof that the product was real, and licit. The reporter spoke again into the microphone.

"That's our strange news item of the day. Now, back to our studios."

13

C6

The Trouble with David

It was quarter to six in the morning and the phone rang and rang. Still half asleep, AGW picked it up.

"Hello? . . . Here, it's for you. I don't know who it is." She passed the phone to her husband.

"Hello? Who's calling?"

"It's David. You'd better get over here fast. I got big trouble."

From AG's end it sounded like there was a riot going on.

"What? David, my friend! What's up?"

"Hurry, hurry, please get over here!"

AG heard a deafening din of shouts and cries in the background. He hung up and pulled on some clothes. His best friend was in trouble. Maybe a truck loaded with uranium had driven by his vials and there'd been a huge explosion, just as the engineers from Vials & Vials had warned. Or maybe the pyramid of one thousand five hundred bottles had collapsed, releasing thousands upon thousands of minutes and causing cars going by to lose control and unleashing mayhem on the surrounding streets. What was going on?

AG flew down stairs, jumped into his car and raced over to David's store. When he arrived he found a swarming throng: there must have been two thousand people trying to push through the door of the little grocery. Others forced their way out against the surging the crowd. AG couldn't believe his eyes: the people walking by him were holding a familiar item—vials of five minutes!

AG jumped into the crowd, wishing he could just crawl over the people's heads.

"Let me by, let me by, please!"

He finally made it to the door, by now shut tight. Inside he could see his friend, eyes bulging in fear as he stared out at the hysterical mob from behind the counter, like a soldier in a trench watching the enemy bear down upon him.

David thought he spotted AG among the feverish mass of customers howling outside. At the risk of causing an avalanche, he unbolted the door. AG managed to slip in, unable to prevent five or six intruders, who besieged the storekeeper.

"I want a bottle of five minutes!" pleaded one.

"I need it today. Give me one, please. I'll pay any price," begged another.

"You're sold out!?" exclaimed the first.

"How can that be?" said the second with indignation.

"I've been waiting in line since five-thirty this morning!" cried the third.

"It's a disgrace!" they all proclaimed with disdain.

A shove here, a prod there and AG and David managed to hustle the customers back out the door. David
wiped the sweat from his forehead, sat down to catch his
breath, and, having calmed down somewhat, looked AG in
the eye.

"It all started at half past four this morning, when I
came in to bake the bread. The doorbell rang. I thought,
'That's odd.' There were about twenty people outside.
They all wanted the same thing: a bottle of five minutes. I
guess you saw the news last night. I got them to do a report
on your invention. They showed the sign, the bottles . . .
they said my store was selling T. I sold your fifteen hundred bottles in an hour. All morning people have been
coming from all over town. You'd better get back to bottling more of that stuff, and fast, or they'll rip my place to
shreds. Here, take this." David handed AG $2,250, his cut
for the bottles sold.

AG's heart started pounding. It was as if all his
dreams had suddenly come true. What had started as a
misunderstood pipe dream had now become, literally
overnight, a reality, within his grasp. He saw clearly what
he had to do next. There was no T to lose. It was now or
never! He stood upon the threshold of a whole new life.
He went outside, stood in front of the mass of people
pressing against the door and shouted as loud as he could.

"The bottles of five minutes are sold out! But come back first thing tomorrow morning. There will be enough for all!"

The crowd calmed down and in a few minutes had dispersed. Many were disappointed, for they wanted their five minutes that very day. Come hell or high water, each and every one of them was sure to be back the next morning.

AG couldn't thank David enough; David, for his part, was none too thrilled that his friend had invited all those loonies back the next morning. AG hopped in his car and sped over to Vials & Vials, where the engineers came to the conclusion that the urine bottle was the ideal container, given that there had been no nuclear explosion after twenty-four hours in the container. Since urine bottles came in a single standard size, AG could order as many as he liked. He ordered forty thousand, an order so large that he had sixty days to pay. Plus, with an order that size, the customer could demand delivery in partial lots, however many and whenever he needed them. There was nothing, indeed, like a little buying power. And now AG was working on the strength of his first surge in demand. He loaded a few thousand vials in the trunk of his car so he could start bottling T immediately.

And that's what he did. However, with only twenty alarm clocks production would be too slow. But more clocks wouldn't fit in his cramped parking space. He needed space in the garage to increase the number of bottling lines. The logical thing to do would have been to look for another place to set up shop, but AG hadn't the T. Besides, Hewlett-Packard had spent a few months in their garage before moving to more conventional premises. Not one to be outdone, he went to see all his neighbors in the building and for an affordable price acquired all the parking spaces in the garage. He used all the $ he earned on the first day of sales to make the down payments, with the promise that they would sign before a notary public in one month's T, when he expected to have enough liquidity to pay off the remainder of the agreed price. He took possession of all the parking spaces except the one belonging to the neighbor from 4B, who, we might recall, had run off to live with Dr. Che, and thus AG had been unable to deal with her. In any case, he needed the space so that AGW would still have somewhere to park. Just as well.

AG delivered all the vials of T David asked for. But—and this was the surprising thing—orders for bottles of five minutes were now coming in from all over the country.

AG needed to hire workers for Freedom, Inc. It wasn't difficult to find people, rather it seemed every jobless person in the neighborhood came knocking at his door. They showed up in droves. Apparently there wasn't a soul around who hadn't heard about his success with bottled T.

The organizational bit was easy. Out of every four neighbors he took on, he assigned one who had his or her own vehicle to deliver vials to retailers, the second to buy alarm clocks, the third to print labels, and the fourth to man the bottling line in the garage.

So, in just a few days, AG had two thousand alarm clocks, two million urine bottles and a million and a half stick-on labels. All that thanks to a small army of two hundred and forty local residents ready to produce as many bottles of T as he needed.

The orders came in by phone to AG's home, where the line was permanently busy. He hired his mother-in-law to take orders, while AGW stayed in the garage by the light switch, poised to turn the lights back on every time they went off and keep the bottling line on the go.

The next days were madness. The garage swarmed with workers running along rows of alarm clocks and empty vials being filled with T one after the other. As soon as the vials were filled, they were loaded into the Freedom, Inc. delivery vehicles and rushed off to their destination.

They tried to keep things running as smoothly as possible, but it was difficult, given that the staff he'd hired had no experience in bottling T. There were moments when AG lost his patience.

"Can't you see that those vials have been filling for ten minutes!? You think we're in the business of giving away T for free? Get a move on! Another set of vials! Careful with those vials, they're going to . . . spill! Would you please sweep up those minutes from the floor . . . yes, yes . . . are you blind, or what? More labels! More vials!"

Throughout the month, the papers carried front-page news about AG's enterprise.

Unnamed Settled Area Today
Boom in demand for five-minute vials

The Half Truth
*Can Freedom, Inc. keep pace with demand
for five-minute vials?*

Our Impartial Version
Thousands of retailers order vials from Freedom, Inc.

They Say It Happened
Product-of-the-year sales continue to surge.

Demand was strong, to say the least, and hundreds of markets remained untapped. If he played his cards right, AG would be a millionaire in a few months. That is to say, the Rd-Hded Trmtes were now almost within his grasp.

C7

T Consumption

A pack of cigarettes, a box of matches, and a bottle of five minutes, please," ordered a woman in a drugstore.

"Oh my, I must have walked out the door without my five-minute vials! Can you lend me one till tomorrow? I promise to pay you back," one friend commented to another on the metro.

"You're always mooching my T!" came the reply.

"Did you know that Paula still hasn't tried the five-minute vials?" whispered one employee to another, standing by the coffee machine at work.

"Oh, you know, she's a bit weird."

"Victor, whadda ya say we do five minutes at noon?" suggested an office colleague.

"You're on! See you down at the coffee shop."

All citizens were free to use their vials as they wished. The five-minute vials of freedom were the perfect product. People had a need for T for themselves. And that was precisely the need satisfied by the product that AG had conceived.

More and more bottles were being sold everywhere across the country. Millions of people bought and consumed the five-minute vials. It was the hottest item in the shops. Who hadn't tried the five-minute vials of freedom?

The papers were flooded with letters from readers from all walks of life giving thanks and offering praise for AG's idea. The vials of T changed the lives of nurses, street sweepers, barbers, van drivers, pilots, office workers, secretaries, teachers, civil servants. . . . People felt much less dependent on the system, and they were happier. As one might expect, a large chunk of the consumption of T occurred during working hours. The entire population of the Unnamed Settled Area experienced the happiness of owning their own T and, at any moment—at the office, at the shop, or at the factory—of being able to stop what they were doing and consume five minutes.

Some used their T to take a snooze at the desk; others, to play solitaire on the computer without worrying about the B sneaking up behind them. Couples who worked near each other would synchronize their watches in the morning and take their T together; they'd meet on the street, pop open their bottles and smooch for five minutes, something no couple had had T to do before, not during the week, at least.

The employers were caught off-guard. If an individual purchased and consumed T, such T of course belonged to the said individual, but it was also evident that, if consumed during working hours, such T was committed to the employer. Who had priority? Being that this was something a person bought, the resulting ownership rights had to be recognized, and in no case could such rights be denied. Indeed, it could be argued that the T one bought was not the same T one had committed to one's employer, but rather another T altogether. The coincidence of the bottled T and the moment of consumption was pure chance, and one thing had nothing to do with the other. Although they accepted this thesis, the employers alleged that they could not pay for minutes not worked, and proceeded to deduct any T consumed during working hours from paychecks. This meant that the people of the Unnamed

Settled Area had to accept that buying T meant earning less $. But as people consumed only one or two bottles a day, the impact on their monthly income was hardly perceptible. No T user noted a significant decrease in buying power.

Contrary to what one might expect, the employers raised no further objections; rather, they gradually discovered the benefits of their workers' buying T. While it was true that the intermittent absences of employees at unforeseen or unplanned moments did require slight adjustments along the line, this found compensation in an extraordinary increase in worker motivation and improved work environment. The rates of absenteeism and work hours lost due to colds or flu dropped by more than half. People no longer had to feign illness to get a break from the daily grind: they only had to open a couple of vials, any T of the day.

So it was that one fine day Freedom, Inc. got a call from a factory.

"We want to place an order for bottles of T for our employees."

"What's that you say?" AG's mother-in-law exclaimed. "But . . . doesn't it bother you that your employees consume T during their working hours?"

"Well, you see, consuming T is a right no worker can be denied. Why should anyone, just because they forgot their vials at home, be deprived of a bit of T? It would be counterproductive for our business if, at a given moment, a worker were unable to consume a vial of T. That would raise the stress level. You can't imagine how much the work environment in our factory has improved. The number of strikes and protests has dropped dramatically since the workers have started to consume T."

And that was only the first case, for soon legions of businesses were ordering vials of T to sell out of the refreshment and coffee vending machines on their premises.

Vials of T were also sold in all sorts of establishments. The cafés that had rejected them months before, the discount marts that had underrated them, the vending machines in the metro, and all the other stores that wanted to hold on to their customers, all of them ended up selling the bottles of T.

For their part, the authorities didn't pay much attention to the T business. They just checked that the patent existed and that AG had all the necessary permits and licenses. Seeing that everything was in order, they did nothing else about it, except to send out a tax inspector.

Success had not dulled AG's keen mind: he gave the inspector so many vials that the latter had no T to inspect Freedom, Inc. and returned no more; nor did he ever return to his desk at the Homeland Revenue Service—

where his former bosses, concerned that they might run out of inspectors, opted not send anyone else either.

And the political establishment? It spoke in one voice—in favor of T sales. The popular enthusiasm for the five-minute vials was such that politicians (how could it be otherwise!) tried to take the credit for themselves. Both sides, government and opposition, issued a constant stream of declarations in favor of granting Freedom, Inc. whatever facilities it might need in order to raise production and broaden its distribution of bottled T to every corner of the country. There were even congresspersons who claimed that the vials of T constituted a product of national interest, and so were deserving of official protection.

The months went by. More and more vials left AG's garage headed in every direction around the country. To bolster production, AG filled the garage with more and more alarm clocks, and it got to the point where there simply wasn't the space to grow any more. The clocks were stacked one on top of the other and the rows of bottles to be filled with minutes were crowded perilously together.

"Honey, I think the T has come to move," AGW said to her husband one day.

"You're right, we've run out of room. There are too many people, too many clocks, and too many vials on the floor. . . ."

"Oh, not because of that, it's because I can't find an electrician to fix the garage lights. I've been standing over there by the door switching them on twelve hours a day for months now."

AG set out to find new premises. He needed a big place, with enough space for offices and T-bottling lines, and lots of room to grow. He also wanted to build a warehouse for the millions of vials that he planned to produce in the coming years. And he needed somewhere to park delivery vans; it had become imperative to have his own fleet of vehicles to deliver the bottles of T.

AG looked high and low before finding the right place, on the outskirts of town, in a spot where he could grow as far as the eye could see, on the edge of thousands of miles of desert just waiting to be developed, whenever he was ready.

Once he had the deed to the land and had secured the building permits, AG met with the five engineers from Vials & Vials and gave them a mission.

"I want a flagship factory."

The engineers joined Freedom, Inc. They designed and built a mechanized bottling plant that operated "like clockwork." Never better said! The plant consisted of fifteen sheds, each over two hundred yards long, in which thousands upon thousands of alarm clocks all ticktocked away in perfect unison. Every five minutes, all the alarm clocks rang at precisely the same moment and a mechanical arm capped and sealed the urine bottle, thus ensuring the correct bottling of five minutes of T.

Next, a conveyor belt carrying the bottles activated automatically and carried them in single file to the labeling room, where another machine stuck on the labels with the logo and instructions for use. The vials were then carried on another belt to the warehouse and, without delay, another set of empty bottles entered. And the process started all over again. Everything automatic. What a thrill to see the bottles moving smoothly from one conveyor belt to another! The sight was truly amazing: the factory of freedom was a shining example of industrial acumen, a model for the rest of the world to follow. They christened the factory *Modern Times*. A massive sign on the front, inspired by the Vials & Vials slogan, proclaimed: *Not a minute more, not a minute less.*

And what a good slogan it was, bearing in mind that to put a drop too much T in a bottle meant lost profits, while a drop too little would sully the good name of a company that boasted of never having received a complaint for an underfilled vial.

With the new factory, production grew from thirty to two hundred bottling lines; the company bought a fleet of two thousand vehicles. Freedom, Inc. continued hiring more and more people until it had a workforce of two thousand.

Almost all the workers at Freedom, Inc. were from AG's neighborhood. The unemployment rate in his district dropped to zero. Paradoxically, that formerly jobless mass now produced all the T the rest of the population consumed. The factory's workers didn't have the same dependence on the system as the rest of the population, because they got the product they bottled—T—free. In other words, they could have as many bottles of T as they wished. The very idea that they could have it whenever they liked suppressed their appetite for T. So, oddly enough, Freedom, Inc. was the only company in the country whose workers hardly consumed bottles of T. They had grown sick of T, just as the workers in a soft drink bottling plant would grow to abhor cola.

As well as his workers were getting on, AG was aware that he needed to put his personnel management into the hands of a professional. He contacted his old HR-Drctor, who immediately agreed to come over to Freedom, Inc. AG liked having him around: mornings in the company cafeteria they chatted about beetles, Trmtes, and other insects.

By now Freedom, Inc. had grown into a huge operation, a mammoth producer of T. But that wasn't enough for AG. In terms of sales figures he was aiming so high now that he decided to launch a TV advertising campaign. When he learned how much twenty seconds of air-T cost and compared that with how much he earned per vial sold, he calculated that twenty seconds on TV was equal to his profits for about twenty-five thousand minutes. Outraged, AG decided to come up with an ad the networks would air for free.

"Impossible," everyone told him.

But for AG nothing was impossible. He thought about it for a week before he hit on the solution.

The spot was simple: a gentleman dressed in black, against a white background, would appear on screen with a well-filled five-minute bottle made to look extremely appetizing. Then he'd speak into the camera.

"I'm going to take the five minutes of T in this vial. I'll be right back. . . ." And as soon as he opened the vial the next ad would come on. And then, after five minutes of ads for other products, the gentleman in black would reappear, hold up the now empty vial and exclaim,

"How wonderful it is to consume T! Buy Freedom's vials."

So, five-second slots, when the standard ad lasted twenty or thirty seconds. In other words: advertising dirt cheap!

But the most astonishing thing was that the viewers actually waited through five mind-numbing minutes of ads to see if the guy with the vial would really return as promised. No one, absolutely no one changed channels; they even bet on whether the guy would come back or not. And so AG's campaign put an end, once and for all, to ad zapping.

The networks were all falling over themselves to get the ad and place it at the beginning of their ad breaks and so keep their viewing audiences glued to their sets, something that hadn't happened in a long T. Competition among the networks for the Freedom, Inc. ad flared to the point that, just as AG had predicted, they were soon offering to run the spot free.

AG also determined to set up a sales department: his mother-in-law was still taking orders from her apartment. She loved to talk on the phone, but after several months of twelve-hour days on the horn she decided she'd had her fill, and had her phone cut off. AG's father-in-law was now without a phone and had to get a mobile phone, something he had never imagined doing.

Thereafter, orders were handled by the sales department, located below AG's office. They took orders for T by phone, fax, e-mail, and every available means. AG named his friend David sales manager: as the first T seller in history, he had the track record to make him just the man for the job. David set up a team of four hundred salespeople who took orders from stores and other establishments nationwide.

His mother-in-law was no longer needed and took early retirement. At a moving farewell dinner offered by all her colleagues, they presented her with a gold alarm clock.

But the most extraordinary event of that eventful year happened on its last day: the President of the Unnamed Settled Area mentioned the bottles of T in his New Year's Eve address.

"AG, turn on the news!" his wife cried breathlessly. "Everybody's saying that the President is going to talk about you!"

AG switched on the TV in his office. As he did every year, the President reviewed the most important issues and events of the year for the country. Toward the close of his address he said, "The fact that a country grants its citizens the freedom to consume their own time is only a sign of the maturity of a society."

AG took a deep breath, tears welled up in his eyes. From his grand office of six hundred and fifty square feet, (or a thousand for friends), he proudly contemplated the three hundred and twenty-five thousand square feet of bottling plant running at a furious pace.

He lay back on the leather couch facing the TV and said to himself,

"I did it."

Ever More T for All

c8

H ad nothing else occurred, nothing else would have occurred. But that's not how it was, and this is what, in fact, did occur: the citizens of the Unnamed Settled Area weren't satisfied with a few minutes of T a day, and Freedom, Inc., in its quest for limitless growth, replaced the five-minute bottle with a new product: the two-hour carton, which turned out to be a rousing success.

The habits and patterns of T consumption of the inhabitants of the Unnamed Settled Area underwent radical change. The per-person consumption rate shot up to one two-hour carton a day. There were those who preferred theirs first thing in the morning, thus arriving at work two hours late. Since people could then sleep in the next morning, this facilitated a higher rate of lovemaking, the result being a 20 percent jump in the birthrate in Unnamed Settled Area, which for years had been negative. Other folks chose to consume their two-hour dose in the middle of the workday, taking advantage of the T to play tennis or to attend yoga class and returning to the workplace fresh and rejuvenated. Absenteeism continued to drop. Going to work was a pleasure, for it meant having a couple of hours for whatever one wished. Indeed, if you didn't go to work . . . you sacrificed your free T! Then there were people who consumed their two-hour carton in the afternoon, during the last two hours of the workday, and thus were able to personally assume tasks they hadn't had T for in years, like picking up the kids at school or visiting family and friends.

In a span of three months, AG multiplied his billing twelvefold and, accordingly, the number of minutes he produced and sold around the country each day. To meet such a rise in demand, AG implemented a proportional increase in the number of bottling lines. Freedom, Inc. grew from three hundred and twenty-five thousand to one million seventy-five thousand square feet, and from two to six thousand employees.

The sales of the bigger and better T container brought still greater joy to the inhabitants of the Unnamed Settled Area. Not everyone, however, was so happy. While the five-minute vials posed no serious problems, the two-hour carton was wreaking chaos on the workplace. Whenever someone tried to find a colleague to deal with some matter or another, as often as not the person would be out, consuming that daily carton of two hours. Of course, progress slowed, problems lingered on unsolved, and decisions that had once taken a few minutes were now put off for days.

A story went around about an executive who took over a month to dictate a letter to his secretary, because every time they got started she would take her two-hour carton of T and go off to tai chi class, as was her inalienable right to do.

Given the situation, employers had no choice but to hire more staff, to cover posts that, without any warning at all, were suddenly found vacant.

The business community was up in arms. It was an outrage! You couldn't let people use their T in any way they wished! Five minutes was one thing, but two hours . . . that was a whole different story!

A secret meeting was convened, and representatives from business, finance, and the government came. A businessman addressed the man from the Gvmnt.

"The situation is unsustainable, we must do something. Every company in the country has seen its production costs skyrocket because of this lunacy. When production costs rise, prices rise. When prices rise, sales fall—and exports. When sales fall, earnings fall. And when earnings fall, the government loses revenue. You'll see how corporate tax revenues sink like a stone. It's not just a problem for business; no, this concerns the government too."

"However," replied the man from the Gvmnt, "companies are hiring more people. There is a huge drop in unemployment. You might even say it no longer exists. Since more workers have been required to redress the continuous absences among the workforce, employment offices have been recording almost zero unemployment for the first time in years. The government believes that the two-hour cartons have wiped out unemployment in the Unnamed Settled Area once and for all. Do you not think that wealth is being redistributed?"

"That may be, we don't deny it. But you'll see how it hurts the country in the long run. This man . . . what's his name? Ah, yes, AG! This fellow who has caused a national crisis. . . . He'll get what's coming to him," an exasperated industrialist answered.

Another spoke gravely.

"What we cannot accept is that we deduct from workers' salaries only the cost of the hours they consume while they remain absent from their posts. Much more must be deducted, much more than what we pay for a minute of work. The *fair* solution would be to deduct the profits that two hours of work produce. That would allow us to recover part of the lost productivity."

"How much are we talking about?" asked the Gvmnt man.

"We are talking about multiplying the salary deduction that we currently apply for each minute a worker consumes tenfold, which is the average productivity per hour per person in this country."

The Gvmnt rep took exception to the proposal.

"Are you quite out of your mind?! Do you want to start a revolution? Don't you realize, man, that, after all, it is the workers themselves who pay for the hours consumed? We cannot ask a person to lose ten times more per hour than he does now! That would be unfair."

"What other solution do we have? Is there any alternative?"

"We could ban sales of T. We had considered petition-ing the Gvmnt to amend the law," suggested one of the bankers.

The Gvmnt man slammed the table with his fist.

"What?! But . . . do you not recall that not a year ago the President, in his New Year's address to the nation, said, and I quote: "The fact that a country grants its citizens the freedom to consume their own time is only a sign of the maturity of a society." You yourselves, our business leaders, said to anyone who would listen that T sales contribute to keeping the peace in our society and help reduce absen-teeism in the workplace. What we cannot do now is hold that it should be illegal to sell T, merely because too much of it is consumed. The sales figures for a product cannot be used as a reason for taking it off the market. It's either yes or no. And if it's yes, it cannot be half yes, or in the cases that you gentleman so choose. If we have allowed our free citizens to buy T, we cannot now place limits on that freedom just because they consume a lot of it. You would not oppose their buying three times as many cars, would you? You never complained when people decided to have two or three televisions, did you? No one says how many packs of cigarettes a person can smoke a day, do they? Don't you see?"

Another businessman sighed, then spoke.

"Calm down, gentlemen, please! If we can neither ban the sale of T, nor charge more $ for people's T, the only thing we can do is to ask everyone to at least make use of their two-hour cartons at the same hour of the day. Utter bedlam reigns in the workplace. When one production-line worker isn't off, another is. This last week, on a flight, two passengers had to man the refreshments cart because the flight attendants opened a two-hour carton after takeoff. Club owners say that people now dance without music, because their DJs consume T like crazy. Do you realize that the other day they broadcast the TV news by candlelight because the lighting crew had taken a two-hour carton to celebrate the birthday of one of the writers?"

The Gvmnt man reflected on the implications of this proposal for a moment before replying.

"If we oblige each and every citizen to consume his or her two hours of T at the same hour of the day, it will be interpreted as a shortening of the work day and what is being sold here is freedom. People buy their T because it belongs to them. Or are you, gentlemen, the ones to decide when people have to consume what they buy with their own $? That would hardly differ from your decreeing that everyone must take their coffee break together. Preposterous. Let me suggest another solution. I shall pose the problem to the Secretary of the Economy. Where I do agree with you gentlemen is in that the day may come when Freedom, Inc. becomes a grave threat to the economy of the country. We'd best be on our guard. I shall prepare a plan for the expropriation of Freedom, Inc. When the T comes to stop AG, I'll have everything ready for us to take over his business and regulate T sales, but for the T being we must wait. In my view, that moment has not yet arrived."

The meeting ended and the Gvmnt representative began to devise a plan to deal with Freedom, Inc., should the moment arrive when its activities posed a real threat to the nation's economy. Although he had tried to hide it from the businessmen, he was, in fact, quite concerned. Was it really the moment to intervene, as the businessmen and Bks claimed?

Meanwhile, far away, quite unaware of the plot being hatched against him, AG called a meeting of his top management on the south side of the immense Freedom, Inc. industrial complex. The day was hot and the five engineers, David, and the HR-Drctor stood under the scorching sun, waiting expectantly.

"Why did you bring us here?" asked one of the engineers from Vials & Vials.

AG breathed in and, scanning the horizon, spoke.

"You've all seen the works going on to the south, behind this fence. You also know that what we've been building is supposed to be Termiteland, the place I've always dreamed of, the thing that drove me to found Freedom, Inc."

His chiefs of staff nodded. AG was referring to massive earth-removal works that for weeks had seemed only to fill the air with dust. Two hundred excavators dug up earth and more earth in what looked like a strip mining operation. In the company lounge, it was rumored that it would be the biggest theme park on the planet, with space for more than five hundred million Trmtes.

"That is not so," AG revealed. "Termiteland will be a reality, but this is not where I will build it. What these two hundred sheds contain are not Trmte terraria. They are T-bottling plants: production lines with thousands and thousands of alarm clocks. I have had a vast workforce bottling T every day, nonstop, for the last four weeks. In fact, I have multiplied our T-production capacity by a factor of two hundred. I inform you that we have millions of minutes in our stockpiles."

"But where have you put all that T?" asked the five engineers in unison.

"They're right! Where is it being kept, if we don't have the capacity to store that amount of T?" the personnel director asked.

"They're in the silos," AG answered with an air of triumph.

"The silos?" David's eyes widened in surprise.

"That's right. I had the site dug up; I have built a series of underground silos, hundreds of thousands of cubic feet in capacity, to store billions of minutes in bulk. At this very moment, the silos are chock-full of T. They hold millions upon millions of hours ready to be sold."

His chiefs-of-staff could barely believe their ears. What was AG thinking of doing with all those minutes? But he didn't give them T to formulate the question; he produced a package from behind his back.

"This, gentleman, is our newest product: the one-week magnum!" he exclaimed enthusiastically.

The great advantage of buying T by the week took a moment to sink in, then AG's chiefs-of-staff clapped and cheered with glee. Truly, AG was a genius. They had proposed continued growth and he had come through. The idea was absolutely brilliant. If people had gone from the five-minute vials to two-hour cartons, how could they fail to move up to one-week magnums?

Before the first units were distributed to the stores, the news was leaked to the media.

Unnamed Settled Area Today
Freedom, Inc. to launch one-week packages of T.

The Half Truth
The one-week magnums will cost a quarter of a month's salary. Will people be willing to buy them?

Our Impartial Version
AG seems to know no bounds. He now wants people to buy his T by the week.

They Say It Happened
It's madness. AG goes too far this time.

But it wasn't madness at all. The inhabitants of the Unnamed Settled Area, who were well trained in consumption, went wild for the one-week magnum, buying one a month. Demand rose day by day, exceeding all expectations, and Freedom, Inc. was hard-pressed to keep up.

Monday morning people arrived at work and showed the B a one-week magnum.

"See you next Monday. I'm off to the country for a week."

Now, that was freedom! It was beyond anyone's dreams. With the one-week magnums, Freedom, Inc. now offered days and days of T for oneself. People paid more for their T than what society would have credited them for, such was their desperation to recover what was, in fact, theirs.

But the resulting anarchy in the workplace grew exponentially. One might well imagine the implications of a situation in which, without warning, anyone could take a one-week leave of absence. The magnums had only been on the shelves for a few weeks: what would happen when the entire population of the Unnamed Settled Area was buying a week of T every month? Could the country continue to function? One thing was for sure, if everybody bought the magnums, the turnover at Freedom, Inc. would be equivalent to a quarter of the sum of personal income for the entire country. When AG held that proportion of the gross national product of the Unnamed Settled Area he would wield more power than the Gvmnt and all the Bks in the country put together.

But that day would never come, because neither the Bks, nor the private sector, nor the Gvmnt were willing to let it come. The T had come to stop Freedom, Inc. Things had gone too far. The Gvmnt representative, after a secret meeting with businessmen and the Bks, was now trying to convince the Secretary of the Economy of the Unnamed Settled Area to expropriate Freedom, Inc.

"Mr. Secretary, not long ago the sale of two-hour cartons started to cause a few problems, but now the situation has become unsustainable. Since the launch of the one-week magnums, private-sector profits have taken a nosedive. Industry, trade, services . . . without exception all the businesses in the country are suffering a severe drop in productive capacity. For a T they were able to cover for absent workers by hiring more personnel, but that was before—now there is no unemployment. It's a disaster! We have a labor shortage, because there's no one left to hire!"

The representative continued, "Moreover, the problems do not end there. A worker who consumes a week of T takes home twenty-five percent less at the end of the month. And that means a crippling decrease in the buying power of the public."

The Secretary listened gravely.

The representative went on. "That's not all. The one-week magnums are also causing a banking crisis. With people earning less, their savings accounts are being drained. Average savings have dropped by half. People are living on half of what they used to have in the Bk. If people don't earn enough, they won't be able to pay off their loans and mortgages. The system depends on loaning them $ so they will then devote all their T to working for the system. We can't afford to let people own their own T, or we all go to hell! We face grave danger! Freedom, Inc. has put the idea into people's heads that, given more free T, they needn't consume so much. People are being enticed to stop consuming!"

He summed up the series of problems facing the country. "In sum, we have no labor pool, bad debt is up, savings down, personal income down, and a culture of nonconsumption is taking hold. We are on the road to disaster! Gross national product will drop thirty percent in the coming months. We face ruin as a country! If profits fall in the private sector, so will state revenue, and that will thwart our efforts to maintain a strong defense, which will in turn put our foreign colonies at risk. With fewer resources in the state coffers we will become vulnerable and other countries could invade us. . . ."

The Secretary of the Economy now spoke. "Still, we can't ban T sales, we'd have a nationwide uprising on our hands. We live in a free-trade society, people can buy whatever they like, even their own T. It's come to the point of no return. What can we do?"

Fortunately, the Gvmnt rep had his evil plan at the ready.

"I have an idea for getting rid of Freedom, Inc. We can expropriate them in a completely legal maneuver."

"How?" inquired the Secretary.

"We know from our sources that AG has billions of minutes stored up in underground silos. All of that production is earmarked to meet the future demand for one-week magnums. If we put a use-by date on all those minutes, Freedom, Inc. couldn't possibly sell them in T. We need to get a law passed to classify T as a perishable good. If we do that, the Freedom, Inc. people will never be able to sell the T stockpiled in the silos, and then they will be starved of liquidity: they won't be able to pay their workers' salaries or pay back the Bk loans they used to build the new plants. Freedom, Inc. will fall into arrears and have to file for suspension of payments, which, given the size of the company, will justify immediate intervention on the part of the state. We will then have the grounds to expropriate. We seize the company. Freedom, Inc. becomes Gvmnt property and we put things back in order."

The maneuver was truly Machiavellian. The Secretary of the Economy smiled.

"OK, start preparing a regulation to impose a use-by date on bottled T. Just like spoiled milk, cheese, or meat, we shall decree that bottled T goes bad too. That would mean his end. We starve AG of liquidity. He'll be bankrupt in less than two weeks."

13

c9

Drums of T

And so, three days later, the Official Bulletin of the Unnamed Settled Area published the following law:

Packaged time expires in fifteen days. After that period no container may be opened or consumed. But if a container of time is opened before its use-by date the owner will be permitted to consume the contents, regardless of the time contained therein.

The new regulation pulled the rug right from under Freedom, Inc., because it did not impede citizens from consuming T, but rather set a deadline for Freedom, Inc. to sell its finished product.

When AG read the bulletin he almost fainted: first he felt queasy, then he started to tremble in his chair, next thing his eyes saw nothing but flashing stars, and finally a cold sweat pulled him back from the verge of collapse.

It was the end. AG knew it. His silos were full of billions of minutes and in fifteen days they'd all be worthless. All that production was earmarked to cover the future demand for one-week magnums, the sales of which had only just begun. And all that T was going to expire. If he couldn't sell the T in the silos, he wouldn't be able to pay his workers or pay off the money he'd borrowed to build the bottling plants. In short, it would all be over in fifteen days. There was no way around it. There was nothing to do. The government had decided to get rid of him. He had become too dangerous. Freedom, Inc. had only few days left to exist. He was ruined. His empire had collapsed like a house of cards. No more Termiteland, no more Rd-Hded Trmtes! It was all over!

AG was shattered. All that hard work, all those ideas that only he had believed in, all that risk, all that investment, all that audacity . . . and the Gvmnt had taken it all away from him. It was dangerous to become important.

He summoned his chiefs-of-staff. They met in the boardroom. They, too, looked crushed. The word had gotten around the factory, and they were well aware that the company had its back against the wall. AG begged them for possible solutions. No one came up with any because there were none. The Gvmnt had plotted against them and won. David sighed, a far-off look in his eyes.

"We have so much surplus T. . . ."

"Indeed, if you divide the billions of minutes that we have by the millions of people in the country . . . that is our surplus T per capita," one of the engineers added.

Before anyone could do the arithmetic, AG spoke.

"That's it! Of course! I've got it! If the T we have in the silos is going to be worthless in fifteen days, then we sell it off and force people to consume it right away, before the use-by date. The new regulation clearly states that anyone who opens a container of T before its use-by date has the right to consume the entire contents, regardless of the quantity. So what we have to do is to get all the citizens of the Unnamed Settled Area to buy an equal share of the minutes we have in the warehouse and make sure that they start taking their T before the fifteen-day legal limit. That means . . . quick, quick, a calculator!"

In a few seconds AG had done his division.

"Thirty-five years! Thirty-five years! If we can sell thirty-five years of T to every man, woman, and child in the country within fifteen days, we'll have sold all the T we have in the silos. We'll have saved the company."

The others could hardly believe their ears.

"But . . . what are we going to put that much T in?" asked David.

"I don't know . . . in drums! That's it! In thirty-five-year drums. Quick! Start buying drums from all the suppliers in the country!"

David posed another disturbing question.

"Wait, wait, AG . . . this is insane. How are we going to get that much $ from our customers? How are they going to pay us for thirty-five years of T that they haven't paid for yet?"

The answer was easy, because in C1 of this book AG faced exactly the same problem: he bought an apartment measuring a thousand, pardon me, six hundred and fifty square feet with thirty-five years of earnings that he had not been paid yet. Thus the solution was clear.

"I see what you mean, David. Nobody could afford thirty-five years of T at our standard prices. We'll have to lower them, we go as low as it takes. Otherwise, only the rich will be able to buy the drums and they already have T. It's all or nothing. We'll have to accept anything of value, whatever each person can give us, and give them a drum in exchange. We'll let them pay us with their homes . . . with whatever they have and are willing to give up. We've got to beat the government at its own game, and to do that we have to own everything. We'll get real estate from the citizens and sell it off. With our returns on the sales we'll pay off our debts. The price doesn't matter, we have to get our hands on everything the people can give us, including their homes."

One of the engineers raised a question.

"And where will people live? What will they live off?"

"Well, I guess that people who have all their T for themselves will go live in the country, in tents, in public parks, I don't know. . . . In any case, I'm sure people will buy all that T, because everyone has to recover the T they've sold. I guess they'll come up with a new parallel economy."

"I can't see it, I can't see it. . . . How are the outlets going to handle the drums? They'll be too big to fit in stores," the HR-Drctor said.

But AG had an answer for everything.

"That's a good question. Just this once, we'll dispense with the conventional channels of distribution. We don't have the T to distribute drums through retail outlets. We'll take direct orders by phone from the public and ship the drums directly to people's homes. We'll take everyone off the production lines and set up two of our sheds with desks and chairs; we'll put in cordless phones and have a main board to distribute the incoming calls."

The HR-Drctor had another question.

"But . . . are you saying that when someone gives us their home to get their thirty-five years, we'll put them out on the street?"

"Well, yes . . . but only when we need to sell to get the liquidity. Remember that the Bks will make us keep up with the mortgage payments on the property people give us. But . . . enough questions! You are the ones who should be giving the answers. Get back to work! We don't have much T. Within fifteen days the millions of minutes that we have in our silos will be worthless."

And so AG prepared to launch the product that would save him from the Gvmnt's ploy. Had it been up to him, there would have been no need to launch such a large package of minutes, but they'd given him no choice. Besides, now he knew what he'd do when he had all that $. Termite-land would look like a toy compared to what he would build with the $ he would earn from the new product.

AG had outflanked the authorities. How could they stop him now? The marketing of the thirty-five-year drums was perfectly legal, in compliance even with the diabolical T expiration rules published the preceding day.

The next day, when people went out to buy T, they found there was none to be had. All the stores, bars, restaurants, and other outlets had the same sign up:

To buy more T call Freedom, Inc. at 999-555-444-333. As of today, T will only be sold directly over the phone.

On the first day of drum sales, calls started coming in at eight in the morning and by eight-thirty the switchboard was lit up like a Christmas tree.

Like its predecessors the five-minute vial and the two-hour carton, and just as the one-week magnum had started out, the new thirty-five-year package was a rousing success.

People surrendered to Freedom, Inc. the deeds to houses, apartments, and all sorts of other properties to get their hands on thirty-five years of T, because what good did it do to save up for thirty-five years if, when the T came to enjoy it, you hardly had any life left to live? To be free, you had to give everything to Freedom, Inc.

As the company received property, T was removed from the silos. From there it was put into plastic drums in exact thirty-five-year doses, which were delivered directly to the people who had ordered T by phone, and who would never return to work—because, of course, their T now belonged wholly to them.

Meanwhile, all the other employers scrambled to hire more workers to replace the people who were taking the next thirty-five years off, but no one replied to their ads, because everyone was busy buying their drums and would no longer have T for anything but themselves. How could the country continue to produce goods and services if no one was willing to work for the next thirty-five years?

One by one, AG dealt with the demands for $ from the Bks of the country, who, upon notification of a change in ownership on the real estate they held in their mortgage portfolio, would then send the corresponding mortgage payment-due slip to Freedom, Inc. For the T being, the company had the cash to meet the payments promptly.

But a large number of Freedom, Inc. workers were transferred from bottling, where they were no longer needed, to real estate sales. That supplied the company with the liquidity to keep pace with the payments on the enormous volume of assets that it was adding to its holdings.

Activity at Freedom, Inc. was frantic. Orders for thirty-five years were taken and delivered in drums, demands for million $ payments came in from the Bks and real estate was sold to make the payments.

AG's scheme was going as planned.

But fourteen days later disturbing calls started coming in from the real estate salespeople that AG had sent out to cover the country.

"No one's buying apartments!" one said.

"We're not getting any calls from home buyers! What's going on?" another lamented.

"Why doesn't commercial property sell anymore?" asked another agent, trying to suppress his anxiety.

This indeed represented a real problem: if they couldn't sell the properties, they wouldn't be able to pay off the mortgages on the real estate Freedom, Inc. still held. Just why this was happening was easy to explain: in the first days after the launch of the thirty-five-year drums a relatively small proportion of the population bought them. Many people were still in a position to buy the property

that Freedom, Inc. had to sell. Until that point, AG sold his
real estate without much trouble. But of course as more
and more drums were sold, fewer and fewer people
remained with the capacity to buy the property.

Why? Because, in order to buy a house, for instance,
one had to apply for a mortgage. In order to get a mortgage, one had to show that one had certain earnings. And
to have certain earnings, one had to have T to go to work.
But by now, nearly the entire population had already
bought thirty-five years of T. The upshot? There was no
one left with the T to work. And T was precisely what the
people had bought—for themselves. No one could pay off
a mortgage. And that was just what the people who weren't
buying homes were saying.

Freedom, Inc. was in a serious bind. The phones
didn't stop ringing. T continued pouring out of the silos
and into drums to be delivered to customers. And the Bks
insisted on getting the payments on the mortgages they'd
granted. But Freedom, Inc. no longer had the liquidity to
make such payments. Nor did anyone there know where to
get it. Meanwhile, they continued to receive more and
more property in exchange for T. With each call another
piece of real estate was added to Freedom, Inc.'s assets. But
such assets were not liquid—they were only property that
no one, absolutely no one, could buy.

"We need $ urgently. What can we do?" a desperate AG asked David, standing amid the mayhem of the shed where dozens of agents took orders for drums over cordless phones. David was sweating, his tie loose, his shirt open. AG realized then that his world was coming down around him, and he felt like a Wall Street trader standing on the floor on the day of the '29 Crash.

"We could sell more T . . . ," AG suggested, well aware that that was no longer possible.

There was no more T to sell. T had run out. Even if they were to produce more T, no one would buy it. People had acquired just about all the T they had left to live. The market for T no longer existed. Demand had reached its peak and would never rise again. *There was no T left.* Ironically, things had turned out just as the slogan with which AG had embarked on his venture said: *T is running out.* And so it was, T had really run out. It was impossible to sell any more T to anyone.

Suddenly, the shed went silent. The phones stopped ringing. Why? Barely a person remained in the Unnamed Settled Area who didn't already have a thirty-five-year drum. The silos lay empty. It was the fifteenth day since the T expiry regulation had come into effect and AG had succeeded in getting almost the entire population of the country to buy thirty-five years; not a minute remained in the silos.

At this point, Freedom, Inc. owned practically all the real estate assets in the country. The company had no liquidity at all, however, because its liquidity had of course run out before the real estate had. What to do?

Just as the phones in the orders department had ceased to ring, the phones in the payments department started ringing off the hook. The Bks saw that payments promised in recent days were not coming in. Claim after claim jammed the lines. But no $ remained in Freedom, Inc.'s current accounts.

The sale of the thirty-five-year drum had set off a chain reaction in consumption, ending in a silent revolution. The consumption of T had destroyed the consumption of goods and services. What had happened? Was it madness? Was it absurd? No.

When the people of the Unnamed Settled Area saw that their fellow citizens were trading in their homes, they realized that the real estate market was headed for collapse and that no could put them out of their own homes; it would have been impossible to throw the entire country out of their homes. Who could do that?

But there was another reason, a simpler one. One had to unload one's real estate assets, sign the mortgage over to Freedom, Inc., and acquire a thirty-five-year drum ASAP. Why? Because one had to do what everyone else was doing. In any economic system one must have what everyone else wants and get rid of what no one wants, because that is the only way to preserve the value of one's holdings. In the Unnamed Settled Area the drums of T became, in a matter of days, the only accepted means of exchange. Everything else was worthless, because no one wanted it. It was easy to see that the value of real estate would go into a freefall, and so the thing to do was to unload it as fast as one could. And that was what had happened. No one wanted houses or $, just drums of T. And that was the real reason people had traded in their homes.

The system was on the verge of ruin, the industrial society had collapsed. The economy went belly-up. Liquidity was wiped out. There was no workforce, because no one went to work, since everyone had bought their T. And without personal income, there was no demand; nor was there supply, for, without workers, productive capacity was zero. Not only were Freedom, Inc. and individual citizens insolvent, the entire country was too.

AG, with his sales of five-minute vials bottled in a parking space, then with his two-hour cartons, with his one-week magnums, and finally with his thirty-five-year drums, had caused the collapse of the free-market economy that had ruled over the most developed country in the world.

The captains of business met to assess the situation. They had warned the Gvmnt beforehand. But no one had listened. They lamented not having put more pressure on the state when the two-hour cartons hit the market and the situation was still manageable. But the people were now the owners of their T and there was nothing to be done.

Nor did the presidents of the main Bks see any solution. It was only a matter of T before they would have to seek orders for the seizure of assets held by Freedom, Inc. in order to recover real estate now worthless. All that property was the guarantee for the credit they had extended. The Bks had lent millions and millions of $ to the citizens of the Unnamed Settled Area to buy homes. And those homes no longer had any value whatsoever. The Bks, therefore, had lost all their $. How could they recover it now?

The chaos was such that the President of the Unnamed Settled Area himself cut short an official visit overseas. When he entered the meeting room in the presidential residence, he found the Secretary of the Economy, the leading members of his administration, and several generals who sat on what was known as the Crisis Cabinet, which was summoned only under exceptional circumstances. And the circumstances were indeed exceptional. The light was dim in the meeting room. Politicians, top officials, and military men sat tight-lipped. After a few interminable seconds, the silence was broken.

"The situation is truly critical," pronounced the President of the nation. "According to what I've been told, no one in the country shows up for work, industry is at a standstill, the Bks are facing bankruptcy . . . and all because of that moron AG. We should have put a stop to him from the beginning—but he outwitted us. He started off with a harmless product, perhaps even beneficial to society, his little vials of five minutes. But in his eagerness to grow and grow he screwed up the whole world. What drives that man? They say it's Rd-Hded Trmtes. They're to blame for the situation we're in now? My God! I imagine you no longer harbor any doubts that the T has come to do something about Freedom, Inc. We seize the company today. It's a matter of national security. Besides, he doesn't pay his debts. He's billons of $ in arrears."

"Of course we must act," the Secretary of the Economy agreed. "In fact, we have already sent security agents to his home. We do not want him fleeing the country. We await your word, Mr. President, to grant us the authorization to detain him. We shall try him and convict."

"Wait no more. As head of state, I give the order to seize Freedom, Inc. and to bring that SOB to justice. I want to see this Average Guy everyone's talking about behind bars. I want to destroy the man who has bankrupted our country selling bottles full of air. Good Heavens! How could we have been such fools as to let this happen?"

Upon the President's order, the security agents entered Freedom, Inc. and cordoned off the premises. They then proceeded to detain AG and bundle him into a police car: he would be accused of high treason and tried by a military tribunal.

C10

The Gvmnt's A & L

One week later . . .

"The breakdown has affected a large part of the system and the blackout may last a while. We're sorry, but until we can repair the system, we cannot execute you. There has to be sufficient power to cause cardiac arrest and the emergency backup system may not do the job."

The prison official's explanation was eloquent enough to dash all hopes of the delay having something to do with a possible reprieve for AG. He might have guessed. If he couldn't offer the President a solution, there would be no commuting his death sentence. But what could he do? He had no T. No. No matter how hard he thought about the problem, no solution occurred to him. The trial had been quick, for under the state of emergency in the Unnamed Settled Area they had tried him in a military rather than a civilian court. AG was judged a traitor to his country, whose economy remained absolutely bust. He was sentenced to death and the judge ordered that he should be executed immediately.

The light provided by the backup system was feeble, but its very existence meant that there was power. So AG, having accepted the inevitable and anxious to get it all over with, made a suggestion.

"How about if I sit down in the chair and we give the thing a try? We have nothing to lose."

"Oh no," replied the priest sent by the penal system to accompany him in his final prayers. "If you don't get enough of a jolt you may suffer a horrible paralysis, which would cause slow death, with you lingering on for some ten years, in the best of cases."

"But," AG insisted, "if I'm paralyzed they can just keep on trying. I don't know much about all this stuff, but I imagine I'll die in the end anyway, won't I?"

"No, no, if you're paralyzed we can't electrocute you. Under the laws of this country it is prohibited to execute paralyzed prisoners. Can you imagine? What an abomination!" the priest retorted in disgust.

"Yes, yes, of course. I don't know how I could have thought such a thing, please forgive me. What will they think of me?"

His feet aching, AG sat down in the electric chair. Straps hung from either side of the chair and the black hood that they would put over his head hung from a hook, next to a black coat belonging to the priest. Meanwhile, the prison official stared at the clock.

"If they don't get on with it, I'll miss the game. Who did you think's going to win? The season's on the line, you know?" he said to AG.

"I thought they'd suspended all sporting events too," AG answered, without much interest.

"Most of them, what with the mess you've created. . . . But today's game is still on."

The jailer stood up from his metal stool and checked his watch again, despite the fact that only a few minutes had passed since last he'd looked. He paced, then fidgeted. No one wanted to wait any longer, but once inside the fateful room, the rules said, they had to wait at least four hours before setting another day and hour for the execution. Only the President could save AG, but it didn't look as if he was disposed to do so.

"Do you want a book to read?" asked the prison official.

"OK, but make it a short one, otherwise I'll die without knowing how it ends."

"How about *The Little Prince?*" suggested the jailer.

"OK, I always wanted to read that but never got around to it. Do I have T?"

"I think so," responded the prison official, querying the priest with a glance.

"Yes, he has T," the man of the cloth answered with irritation.

AG didn't know whether it was his choice of book or the fact that he wasn't dedicating his final hours to prayer that bothered the priest. The truth was that AG had no

regrets—he'd settled his accounts with God quite some
T ago.

The prison official went off to get the book. The priest
and AG remained alone.

"Why? Why did you do it?"

As he raised his gaze to meet that of the priest, AG
saw that in the left pocket of his cassock he carried something cylindrical in shape. He quickly guessed what it was:
a five-minute vial. AG read his thoughts and the priest
looked away, not without a blush.

In that very moment a phone on the wall to his right
rang. Neither the clergyman nor AG knew what to do, for
the official had yet to return. Endlessly, the seconds passed.
The phone continued to ring. Hoping his pardon might
have come after all, AG rose from the electric chair, walked
over to phone, and picked it up.

"Hello?"

"Is that execution room number two? I have the President on the line," said a voice. "He wants to speak with the
prisoner. He wants to make a deal."

The priest looked at him quizzically and made a ges-
ture as if to take the phone, but AG gestured that the call
was for himself. The clergyman sat back down and tried to
hide the plastic vial in his pocket. AG heard a click at the
other end of the line.

At that very moment the prison official returned, *The Little Prince* in his hand.

"His pardon?" he asked.

"I don't know," answered the priest.

AG returned his attention to the phone.

"AG?"

"Yes," he said his heart beating fast.

"This is the President speaking."

Silence followed. They both knew that the call meant a pardon or at least a commuted sentence. T seemed to stop. But AG knew that it was the President who had to speak.

"I want to tell you something. Listen closely."

AG gripped the phone tightly and the President began.

"Bullet, Bugs, Largo, Genius, Astrolabe, Haley, Toto, Thunderbolt, Treasure, Nerve."

He said no more. What was the President trying to say? What was the meaning of that spitfire recitation of meaningless words? Perhaps it was a message in code, a cryptic clue that AG alone could decipher. But he found no meaning in the words, nor did he succeed in discovering the significance of the whole. The President repeated.

"Bullet, Bugs, Largo, Genius, Astrolabe, Haley, Toto, Thunderbolt, Treasure, Nerve."

AG paused, then answered.

"I don't get it. . . ."

Then suddenly he knew what the President had meant: horses. It was the winning combination from last week's races. Swiftly, his mind followed the path that led to a betting slip that, like every week, he'd never placed. It was the exact combination of horses that his father-in-law had asked AG to put his money on. But, how did the President know? What did it have to do with his execution?

AG spoke.

"The ten winners for this week, right?"

"That's correct," said the President.

"And how many hits are there?"

"That's the problem: none. Last week the paper said that the prize wouldn't be awarded, no one bet on all ten winners. There's a million $ pot that wasn't paid out."

The President's intentions were clear. AG's father-in-law would claim the prize and, in all likelihood, they would tell him that no one had placed any such bet. He would then explain his connection with AG, supposing that the bet hadn't been placed because his son-in-law was in prison. The authorities had found out that the slip didn't exist and that, obviously, AG never made the weekly wagers his father-in-law entrusted to him. In other words, the President had the valuable information that AG had been deceiving his father-in-law and keeping the $ from his bets. AG was tempted to explain his motives for doing so, but it struck him as absurd. The President continued.

"We haven't told your family yet. Your wife knows nothing. The Gaming Commission has been putting your father-in-law off with the excuse that they need more T to recheck all the bets. It is your choice to leave this world as a liar and a betrayer of the father of your beloved spouse. I don't suppose you'll want her to spend the rest of her days thinking that her husband, the man she loved so dearly, who was executed in the electric chair, stole from her own father."

In other words, it was blackmail, pure and simple, for AG would never be able to speak with AGW again and tell her how he kept the $ from the horses to compensate for the commission that his father-in-law took under the table from every monthly payment on the mortgage that theirs was the misfortune to have to pay. His wife would remember him as a liar; she would decide to forget him, marry another man, and tell AG-1 and AG-2 their father was a liar.

No. That was too much. He didn't mind dying unjustly for something he was not guilty of, but he couldn't stand the idea of his family, his brother-in-law even, recalling him as a dishonorable man. The President, knowing that AG had by now digested his despicable scheme, went on.

"I want a solution. I want to know how to fix the situation in the country. Otherwise, we'll send out the news. Imagine the headlines: *"AG, executed yesterday, kept the money from his poor wife's father's bets."* You know the government makes the news, however it likes. We'll make your name mud forever. You'll go down in history as a greedy, lying, heartless thief. Your children will have to change their last name and move, probably out of the country."

"Enough! Enough!" That was too much. Much more than AG could stand. But he saw no way out of this new bind. He was trapped. The power would be back on in minutes.

"You think about it," said the President. And he added, "When the T comes, your last moment, you'll have to take stock of your life. I just gave you another item to add to the balance sheet: to be remembered as a common thief. If you don't give me a solution, your life will, in the final moment, come out in the red. I'll be waiting for your call. I am willing to grant you a pardon." The line went dead.

AG slowly placed the phone back on its cradle. Disconsolate, dragging his feet, his arms hanging limp, he returned to the electric chair. Slowly, he lowered himself into it. The priest and prison official regarded him with sadness. AG caught sight of the book the official held in his hands and gestured for him to hand it over. AG opened the little book and turned slowly through the last pages.

He was beaten, resigned to his fate. It was not the proximity of death that grieved him but the memory he would leave in the world. An illustration of the Little Prince under a blinding desert sun carried AG far away from there, to another place. He then read the last lines in the book.

> Here, then, is a great mystery. For you who also love the little prince, and for me, nothing in the universe can be the same if somewhere, we do not know where, a lamb that we never saw has—yes or no?—eaten a rose. . . .
>
> Look up at the sky. Ask yourselves: is it yes or no? Has the lamb eaten the flower? And you will see how everything changes. . . .
>
> And no grown-up will ever understand that this is a matter of so much importance!
>
> —THE END.

At that precise instant, the power returned.

AG buckled himself to the chair. He didn't want them to cover his face, he wanted to meet death face-to-face. They fitted the rest of the straps. The priest made the sign of the cross. The executioner stepped toward the fatal switch. AG began to do the balance sheet of his life and, at that moment, remembered the balance sheet he'd done at home so long ago, the one which had led him to this situation. The prison official stood ready to pull the switch and, a second before the clock struck the hour of his death, AG's face suddenly lit up.

"I've got it! I've got it!" he shouted.

The prison official and the priest both stayed the executioner's hand.

"What's the matter?"

AG was beside himself with excitement.

"I was doing the balance sheet of my life and I discovered the solution to the mess the country's in. Call the President!"

In less than an hour and a half AG found himself being hustled into the Crisis Meeting Room. There sat the President of the Unnamed Settled Area, the most powerful man in the world, well, until two weeks ago, at least. . . .

They sat facing each other. The presidential team— the Secretary of the Economy and various other members of the administration—sat flanking their chief. They all stared at AG, who remained silent and serious. The President spoke first.

"What made you get us into this mess? Why did you do it?"

AG took his T before answering.

"They gave me no choice. If you all hadn't come out with the law about the expiry date for T, I would have gone on selling my one-week magnums for another two years, in peace. Then I would have retired and built Termiteland, and you would have been at the opening ceremony, probably. But of course the system never loses. I had millions of minutes in the warehouse that, thanks to your damn law, were going to be worthless in a few days. What would you have done in my place, Mr. President?"

Silence.

AG continued.

"Besides, if I may, I have something else to say. I'm not the one to blame for all of this. The blame is in the way the system makes slaves out of its own citizens. None of this would have happened if people didn't have to give up thirty-five years' salary to pay for a measly one-thousand, excuse me, a six-hundred-and-fifty-square-foot apartment. I couldn't have a third kid because I couldn't afford a storage space! Don't you realize that you're asking for too much T and sweat for the right to live? I'm not the one who made the bomb; I'm not the one who lit the fuse. The citizens of this country bankrupted the system, not me. The only thing I did was give them the means to do so."

The President and his staff remained silent. The last thing they'd expected was to have to listen to such a diatribe. But AG went on.

"Mr. President, a year and a half ago, I was a bitter man, ground down by a job that had me hiding bills all day every day, slave to a mortgage that I would never be able to pay off, and I took a few minutes to do a balance sheet of my life—my Assets and my Liabilities. My A and my L. Look." AG produced a slip of paper with the figures he'd come up with in C1. He had crossed out the headings over the columns, however.

"You see, the columns are switched around. Since you took over Freedom, Inc. and the company belongs to the State, the Gvmnt owns all the real estate and $ that used to belong to the people. The system owns it all. But it also owes each and every person in the country thirty-five years. The people, on the other hand, have in their assets column all the T they bought and they don't owe anyone anything. Look."

BALANCE SHEET: The System v. AG

A	L
(Has . . .)	(Owes . . .)
All Real Estate	35 years
All vehicles	
All furniture	
All $ in Bks	
All $ under mattresses	
All parking places	

BALANCE SHEET: All Average Guys in the Unnamed Settled Area v. System

A	L
(Have . . .)	(Owe . . .)
Their T	Nothing

The President, the Secretary of the Economy, and the rest of the members of the government realized that the balance of holdings and debts between citizens and the system had shifted—indeed the world had been turned upside down. What was once the system's now belonged to the people: T. And what the citizens once owed, thirty-five years of their T, was what the economic system would now have to wait before having the people at its disposal again.

AG addressed the President.

"Now that it's the system that has the balance that we the people used to have, tell me sincerely: it's tough, isn't it? Don't you find it paradoxical that the system hasn't been able to cope a single week with the balance that the population has been putting up with for years and will have to put up with for many more?"

The President held his tongue for a few seconds. Then he spoke.

"All I want to know is how to restore order. I want people back at their jobs, businesses running again, the $ back in the Bks. If the people don't go back to work I'll call out the army. I'm not squeamish about using force."

But AG interrupted him.

"Are there enough troops left? Remember, they bought their thirty-five-year drums too. . . ."

The President answered sourly, "There aren't many, but enough to bring out the tanks. You got us into this mess and I'm asking you to help us get out of it. I give you my word: I promise to have you pardoned if you tell me how to get people to return to work peaceably. You told me over the phone that you had the answer. Let's not waste any more T. What's the deal?"

"Do you also promise that my father-in-law will get the payoff? My wife will never forgive me if she finds out I've been keeping her father's betting $ all these years. . . ."

"If it works and you get this country out of the hole it's in, I'll give you the payoff right here."

Now then, dear reader, before hearing AG out I shall take the liberty of anticipating his answer, for the only thing able to restore order and peace in the Unnamed Settled Area was in fact the saying from the prologue to this book:

T is $.

Which, as you know, means Time is Money. One only had to look at the new situation in the country: the balances had inverted, so we shall invert the saying too, in other words, $ is T.

In order to function, any economy needs money, and in the people's A-column there was only T; consequently, the only thing to do was to give them $ in exchange for T. In other words, exchange real T for economic T. And this is what AG told the President:

"You have to change the currency. A new currency like this."

He drew something on a bit of paper and showed it to the President.

"Bills and coins of minutes that the government should put into circulation. So you can buy the T back from the people. Pay everyone for the T they have. Give everyone thirty-five years' worth of currency in exchange for the T they hold. When the people have minutes in currency, they'll go back to their old lives. It will be the new currency of the Unnamed Settled Area, T bills and coins. Then, let them buy back their homes with the new currency. And one thing I recommend: don't sell the homes back at thirty-five-year prices, because you'll leave the people penniless again. In fact, if you sell them too high, no one will buy them. You can only inject liquidity in the system if prices are more reasonable, proportionate to the T that people have to give up to buy things."

"And the Bks?" asked the President.

"Well, the Bks lent $ for T. If the new currency is in minutes, they won't have lost $, they'll have lost T. But, that fact remains, that T hasn't passed yet."

The entire Crisis Cabinet, ministers, staff, and President, clapped and jumped up and down whooping with joy. What a genius, this AG! He'd come up with an extraordinarily simple solution that would avoid having to call out the army to restore order. The Gvmnt only had to mint a currency in minutes and the people would exchange the T they'd bought for T in currency form. And the economy would start working again.

The President thanked AG and, right then and there, signed the pardon, his ticket to freedom.

"By the way, I lied to you. Your father-in-law hit the winning combination, but payoff wasn't a million $. It was $5, there were thousands of others who got it right. Here's the payoff." Then he paused and added, "Well, since these $ are minutes now, this is what he deserves."

And the President, blushing somewhat, produced a pre-expiration-date five-minute vial that he'd bought for himself and kept in his jacket pocket. He handed it to AG.

"Friends?"

"Friends," AG answered with a smile.

And they embraced heartily.

TWO ENDINGS

This story has not one ending but two. And that's because this story has not yet occurred, although it will soon, should things continue the way they are.

The first ending is that, just as AG suggested, the people got their T currency, and they bought back their homes at affordable prices. For about two or three years, say. People went back to work and their salaries were paid in minute bills. Things cost what they were worth, which was equal to the T it took to produce them. And life was never so hard again. And it was never again possible to buy things for all the T left in a life.

The second ending is that, after a T, the country was overcome by the fear that people weren't using their T for things that society needed. Someone had the bright idea of putting a tax on something as scarce, and necessary, as water. The price of water went through the roof. Having running water became a luxury, and meant going through institutions known as Water Banks, where people could take out loans. Water became so expensive that you needed a thirty-five-year loan to have it on tap at home. They say that in this second ending, life went back to the way it was at the beginning of this story.

And so it was, after all, that we always end up inventing something to prevent us from being what we can be, for fear that we might become it.

Which of the two endings will turn out to be the real one? It depends, essentially, on each of us. When the day comes, we, the people, will have to work to make it the first.

EPILOGUE

AG's father-in-law wouldn't accept the thirty-five-year bills that the Gvmnt offered him and so he remained without $ forever.

The HR-Drctor returned to the town he grew up in, saved all his T currency, and spent the rest of his life observing the brown-nosed beetle. Only he knew that his hobby was born of an insatiable need to be surrounded by brown-nosers.

David went back to his shop, where he never again accepted another of AG's ideas for new products—perhaps because the latter never offered any.

The five engineers returned to Vials & Vials, where they continued to do calculations that led nowhere, but that justified their high salaries.

The neighbor from 4B returned home to her husband, because Dr. Che steadfastly refused to make love to her.

Aaron, the lawyer who helped AG deal with the paper-work in the constitution of Freedom, Inc., took a long T to get over his disappointment when AG was tried in a military court and he missed his chance to defend the trial of the century.

AG's brother-in-law spent year after year haggling with AG over the rate of exchange between minutes and $ in reference to the cost of the lace curtains. He never collected the debt.

The grade-school teacher never managed to get rid of his stutter and spent the rest of his life teaching half the curriculum dictated by the Department of Education. The school never found out because the students were quite happy to study half as hard.

And AG returned to his home, one thousand square feet to friends and six hundred and fifty according to the plans, where he lived happily with AGW, AG-1, and AG-2, though the latter child is the only one in the family who has yet to appear. But it's always the youngest one in the family that no one pays attention to, and this novel is no exception.

AGW bought a little Trmte farm for her husband, and so he finally discovered that the Rd-Hded Trmte wasn't Rd-Hded at all, but rather blue. Sorely disappointed, he lost all interest in them forever.

END

POST EPILOGUE

When the writer Rosa Regás won the Planeta Prize,* I was driving in my car and I heard her acceptance speech live on the radio. Rosa Regás said,

**"Thank you for this prize.
With this money I can buy something
that is not sold: time."**

When I heard that, I started to wonder what would happen if in a society like ours in the West, time could be bought. The result is this book.

*The Planeta Prize is a prestigious literature award in Spain.

AFTERWORD

I know that this book does not leave the reader indifferent. I have been made aware of this by many of those who have had the chance and kindness to read the original manuscript. They were the ones who suggested that I write this Afterword; especially those who finished these pages in utter despair and depression, feeling helpless in the face of the forces of the system that governs us.

Do not lose faith. This story does not say that change is not possible, but rather quite the opposite. Otherwise, why write it? Is not awareness the first necessary step toward change? Do not slaves observe their masters in order to rebel against them or improve the conditions of their life? *The Time Seller* seeks to awaken all of us who are bound to a routine that has become a source of our alienation.

We should be aware that the economic system in which we live is not sustained solely on money but also on a subtle use of the *time* variable. And we should also understand that this variable must be used with care and caution. The profit motive is the engine that drives people in a free society to undertake initiatives that in turn propel the economy, generate growth, and provide prosperity. On the other hand, the unfettered greed that runs roughshod over more essential matters, over the most basic rights of people—that does not, in short, respect the foundations of the free market system itself—has been the cause of almost all the economic crises that have occurred in history, from the Crash of 1929 to Japan in the 1990s. And, if we fail to avoid it, the same will happen in the twenty-first century. Our reserves of time are, from an economic point of view, running out.

In these early years of the century, the capitalist system has proved itself to be the most efficient from the economic point of view. The communist regimes have fallen one after another, like a house of cards. Development and growth have been shown to be more efficient under a free market system. Adam Smith observed that very thing in the late eighteenth century, when he set out his theory of the invisible hand that directs society toward a different good as each individual receives the benefit of private choices. However, it has taken nearly two hundred years to prove empirically the superiority of this thesis over other paths and alternative proposals. John Stuart Mill, another classical economist, of the utilitarian school, postulated that the objective of the economy was to maximize happiness in the society as a whole. The utilitarians maintained that any shift in the economy should be toward the maximization of the utility of the society as a whole. This is all well and good, but it leads us directly to another question, one not easily answered: How can we measure utility or, still more difficult, happiness?

We need, then, a new frame of reference. The move away from spirituality and the loss of values in the Western world invariably lead to our no longer finding meaning in the things we do. That, among other ways, is how the system has come to own our time.

The economy should assimilate aspects that go beyond the conventional. Erich Fromm posited the problem in his day: "Why is it that a healthy economy is possible only at the price of unhealthy human beings?" The economy is holding out (for now), but many people are not. And let us not forget that it is above all people who sustain the economy. What is happening? We are in urgent need of a utopia to replace those we have lost. There is a crisis of utopias, of that I am sure.

My good friend Mario Alonso Puig, to whom I owe this paragraph, often tells a story in which Fear is the only one that manages to take Love's corpse to the Prince of Darkness. But, like *The Time Seller,* his is only a story. In reality love will always vanquish fear, for the survival of humankind depends on love, despite all the pain and hate we are capable of causing. It is the same for the present system that governs us. It has many positive aspects, but it often goes too far in enslaving us and hurts the very people who struggle to sustain it. If we rank the countries of the world from richest to poorest, and again from highest to lowest rates of depression, we find the order is strikingly similar. We citizens of this world feel the pressing need to free ourselves from the yokes we impose on ourselves to lighten the burden that impedes us from contributing to a better world.

Once again Erich Fromm, in his book *The Fear of Freedom,* describes how the process of "individuation" of the person entails a feeling of loneliness that is only possible to overcome through love for others or creative activity. Otherwise, humans will embrace totalitarian systems, whether they come in the form of unrestrained consumption, state, church, or fascisms.

Today we do not live under political totalitarianisms but rather under another, less tangible one. The system that enslaves us is extremely subtle: we are slaves to our freedom, to our free system. It makes us unhappy, but we accept it because the alternative is no freedom. To rebel against our democracy and the free market would be to rebel against our own freedom. We seem to be trapped in a maze with no way out.

What, then, is the solution? Let us exercise our freedom, but let us give it meaning. Let us seek out our own benefit, bearing in mind that there are ways we can do so while taking into account the needs of others. The system should take from the individual only the time that is fair and absolutely necessary, and it should, in turn, provide each individual with the means to express love, humanity, spirituality, cooperation, solidarity, and help for others. Time is an essential component in our lives and a system that forgets that is destined to fail.

The great economist Xavier Sala-i-Martin (a professor at Columbia University), in his manifold articles and books, has described the capacity of liberalism as a welfare- and wealth-producing system. But he doesn't stop there. He also defines the role of the State in a free society and constantly proposes creative solutions that, while preserving the positive elements of liberalism, facilitate cooperation to redress the inequalities in the world and the abuses that occur when freedom generates externalities, as it inevitably does. And to do that you have to have the courage to swim against the tide and defy the beliefs and actions of the majority.

Gold fever is still with us: the Crash of 1929, the financial crises in Southeast Asia and Latin America, the dot-com debacle, and now time. But the world is full of people with the ability to walk away from the madness and frenzy. This book is no more than an invitation to think and act differently.

That is why I am an optimist with regard to humankind. Because we are destined to survive despite ourselves and we will always look for solutions to the evil that we ourselves—sometimes consciously, other times in ignorance—cause.

I refer back to the words I dedicate to my son Alejo at the front of this book: *"in case I am unable to transmit to him that his time is his alone."* Dear reader, as Gandalf says to Frodo in *The Lord of the Rings:* "All we have to decide is what to do with the time that is given us." Change begins with oneself. Your time is yours and no one else's: live with that in mind and the invisible hand will lead us, once again, to the good of society as a whole.

ACKNOWLEDGMENTS

Books have but one author, but many are those who make them possible.

To my wife, María del Mar, for her unfailing encouragement and the infinite patience she has shown toward me in the gestation of this book.

To Frank Hendrickx, the first person I told this story to, before I had even started writing it. Perhaps he never knew, but our chat on a flight from Athens to Barcelona inspired me in my approach to writing it.

To Ricard Gresa, for his crucial role in the redefinition of the length of the first manuscript and for showing me how I could cut out a good part of it without prejudice to the story.

To Felipe Artalejo, for his generous help in polishing some of the macroeconomic aspects to give the story a certain appearance of reality.

To Emilio Mayo and Álex Rovira for their contributions and advice regarding the first drafts of the story.

To Maru de Montserrat for the time she devoted to revising the successive manuscripts and for her inestimable contributions.

To Gregorio Vlastelica and Carlos Martínez, my editors at Empresa Activa, for their comments and recommendations, and for believing in this project.

To Carmen García Trevijano, a.k.a. *Chituca*, for her tireless labor in the promotion of this book and for the constant joy with which she infects all those who collaborate and work with her.

To Juan Salvador, master of the word, for his suggestions in the revision of this text.

To Joaquín Sabater Sr. and Jr., for their unconditional support for the publication of this book when it was only a project.

To Juan Carlos Tous for his suggestions about AG's character, which helped me define the structure of his personality.

To Juan José Nieto for his sincere comments, which finally convinced me of the need to include an afterword to clarify the intention of this story.

To Carmen Rafel for her words of encouragement and inestimable advice on the publication of this book.

To all the people who read the original manuscript and whose contributions, suggestions, and ideas were in one way or another incorporated into the book: Borja Martín, José Luis Sánchez (Sr. and Jr.), Rosa Castellví, Gemma Lerís, Guillermo and Mercedes Trías de Bes,

Alexandra Llavina, Mercedes Segura, Natalia Lasaosa, Mario Alonso Puig, Ignacio Rafel, and Jordi Nadal.

But, most of all, I want to thank Isabel Monteagudo, because this book never would have been written without her support. There was a moment when, with the manuscript finished, I decided to postpone the publication for a few years. Now I am certain that, if not for her insistence and words of encouragement, it never would have seen the light of day, because I never would have returned to it.

ABOUT THE AUTHOR

Fernando Trías de Bes cofounded Salvetti & Llombart, where he has worked with many top organizations including Bayer, Credit-Suisse, Dannon, Frito-Lay, Hewlett-Packard, Mercedes-Benz, Microsoft, Morgan Stanley, Nestlé, Oxfam, Paramount, PepsiCo, Sony, and Universal. He has also collaborated with consultancies such as McKinsey and Co., AT Kearney, and Bain & Company. He has held marketing positions with several multinationals.

He is coauthor (with Alex Rovira) of *Good Luck: Create the Conditions for Success in Life & Business* (Jossey-Bass, 2004) and coauthor (with Philip Kotler) of *Lateral Marketing: New Techniques for Finding Breakthrough Ideas* (Wiley, 2003). He is a professor of marketing and management at ESADE Business School (Barcelona, Spain), one of Europe's most respected business schools.